Growing Children,
Thriving Children

Testimonials for Lou Harvey-Zahra

'I love Lou Harvey-Zahra's advice, which is fun but practical, and rooted in love.'

Saffia Farr (editor, Juno *magazine)*

'The ideas in *Growing Children, Thriving Children* have already created more fun and harmony in our family home. I can't thank Lou enough. I consider her my guru of parenting!'

Georgia Bhandari (parent and teacher)

'Lou not only brings keen, valuable insight about child development to teachers and parents, she does it with humour, humanity and heart. She goes beyond philosophy and leaves everyone with the gifts of practical ideas and tools to implement in the classroom and at home.'

Lisa Jordan McCarthy (Dean of Education of Maple Village Waldorf School)

'Lou holds so much wisdom in her heart. I've learnt so very much from her in my parenting journey. *Growing Children, Thriving Children* is a blessing.'

Ilana Karst (parent and Steiner-Waldorf education administrator)

'It is imperative that Lou Harvey-Zahra's message of reverence for children is spread to the far reaches of the globe. Her down-to-earth approach makes ideas accessible to everyone. Lou shows that nothing fancy is required to support the healthy physical and emotional development of children. It really is just about love.'

Cathy Yeoman (parent and Steiner-Waldorf teacher)

'I really enjoy Lou's style. It is her flow, sense of humour and delivery: it is easy to absorb all the wonderful information.'

Jason Freeman (parent)

Growing Children, Thriving Children

Raising 7 to 12 year olds
with confidence and awareness

Lou Harvey-Zahra

Floris
Books

For children, who are the future

First published in 2019 by Floris Books
© 2019 Lou Harvey-Zahra
Third printing 2022

Photos taken by the author

 Also available as an eBook

British Library CIP Data available
ISBN 978-178250-566-2
Printed in Great Britain by Bell & Bain Ltd

Printed on sustainably
sourced FSC® certified
paper. Uses plant-based
inks which reduces
chemical emissions.

Acknowledgements

Thank you to my husband Ged, who is my light and my love. His words are always interwoven within mine. To my mum, Pam, who is my first proofreader and constant supporter. To my friends Sherry and Habib for writing the foreword and for their gift of loving that has spread to so many people. To all the schools, teachers and families around the world that invite me to share my inspirations. And to the parents and children behind the voices and photos throughout these pages.

I am honoured to be given a platform to inspire parents and teachers to enhance the lives of children and families.

Contents

Foreword

Lou Harvey-Zahra's insightful book reconciles the practical and spiritual aspects of being a parent in the twenty-first century. She achieves this by highlighting an important aspect of parenting that most of us are either unaware of or take for granted – our children are here to teach us as much about ourselves as we teach them about the world.

As parents, we know that raising children is as heart-expanding and fulfilling as it is challenging. If we can provide safety and guidance while allowing our children to create their own human experience in a way that transforms them into productive and loving members of society, then we have done our job. But where to start?

Years ago, we read a short poem titled 'On Children' by Khalil Gibran. It emphasises the spiritual sovereignty of children. We were deeply inspired by his description of children as brand-new souls entering this world with the purpose of realising their greatest potential by becoming exactly the people they were meant to be (not who we might prefer them to be). *Growing Children, Thriving Children* touches upon this awe-inspiring grounding process that children must go through to manifest their individual natures and potential. And it encourages parents to embrace their children's unique unfolding, while living each stage of child development.

When we're conscious of our children's divine mission, we understand that our true purpose as parents is to focus on creating *connection*, rather than enforcing rules and regulations. When we approach child-rearing from this perspective, we not only grow in our wisdom and compassion, but our children grow too because they feel seen, heard and acknowledged. These high ideals are fine in principle, but they have to be woven into everyday family life. This is the magic of Lou Harvey-Zahra's writing and presenting style: she is able to help ground this striving in easy-to-apply tips, which appear simple but make a profound difference to children and parents.

Lou provides us with practical ideas, and with a deep understanding of parenting children from 7 to 12 years. *Growing Children, Thriving Children* sheds light on an important stage of our children's lives that is often ignored. Not many books have been written about middle childhood and the pre-teen years. By recognising and understanding the important milestones (or 'Rubicons' as Rudolf Steiner calls them) during this period of development, we as parents can strengthen our connection with our children while reducing the possibility of unnecessary conflict and separation. Lou eloquently illuminates this in her book.

As doctors, we are acutely aware of the need for strong, healthy rhythms, education and prevention: these are the cornerstones to good health. This book is a wonderful source for maintaining family health on a physical, emotional, social and spiritual level.

We met Lou three years ago as she undertook her first book tour of Los Angeles, and were inspired by her passion for parenting, her striving, and her understanding of the true nature of childhood and how to bring holistic family ideas into everyday life. We invited her to be an ambassador for our Love Button Global Movement because her message is one of love.

While recently introducing Lou to an audience here in Los Angeles we compared her words to making a pot of vegetable soup: we all have a variety of vegetables in the fridge, but at times we require a good recipe to make a delicious and nourishing meal. We likened Lou to having a master chef in your kitchen: she will transform the basic ingredients into great connection and communication 'recipes', raising awareness not only for family dinner times, but many aspects of parenting life too.

We are truly grateful that Lou has written about these important middle years of childhood, as it is a vital time to deepen the bond we have with our children. This allows them, as they then go through their teenage years, to spread their wings with more confidence and grace while keeping their orientation toward us as guides – just as the sunflower flourishes while it orients toward the sun.

Growing Children, Thriving Children is a 'must-have' for all parents with children between the ages of 7 and 12, who strive to raise their children consciously, mindfully and lovingly.

Dr Sherry Sami and Dr Habib Sadeghi
Founders of the Love Button Global Movement

Introduction

Growing Children, Thriving Children: Raising 7 to 12 year olds with confidence and awareness has been requested by parents countless times over the past few years:

'I need the next book, Lou – the one for older children.'

'Please write a book on the middle years of childhood!'

My three previous books focus on children up to 7 years. Browsing in the parenting section of a bookshop recently, I easily located books on pregnancy, toddlers and teenagers. But where are the books on the other years of childhood? I agree with parents asking for a middle-years book: there is a gap.

Does this lack indicate that the middle stage is less important than the toddler, young child and teenage stages? You might think nothing much happens from the 7th to 12th years of childhood. But the opposite is true. Ages 7 to 12 represent a very important time of child development. Parents require awareness of their changing child and new ideas and insights to build on the foundation established in early childhood, and to create a strong platform of family connection and communication before the teenage years.

Rudolf Steiner (1861–1925), the influential Austrian philosopher of childhood development and education, believed that the middle childhood years have great significance. He identified three transformation times: one at approximately age 7 with the change of teeth, one at around age 9 that is particularly profound and that is often referred to as 'the crossing' or 'the Rubicon', and one at age 12 marking the beginning of puberty. Each of these ages indicates a shift to a new stage of childhood development. Between the ages of 7 and 12, major changes occur in children's sense of self, their relationship to others, and their grasp of the world around them. This book describes each of these three vital transitions.

When he refers to the transformation at around 9 years, Steiner uses the word 'Rubicon' to indicate the life-changing nature of the transition.

He is making an analogy with Julius Caesar crossing the Rubicon river, the border between Gorde and Italy, in the year 49 BC. Caesar knew that once he crossed the Rubicon, he could never return: he was leaving his home behind. So Steiner indicates that children cross a personal Rubicon: they take a step into the next phase of their being and cannot return to the way they experienced life in early childhood. We see evidence of the 9-year Rubicon changes, for example, in children's imaginative play, in their sense of time and in their growing independence.

In my workshops, I ask parents to imagine that children are crossing a bridge from one stage of development to the next. Children leave their present childhood world and step across to a new shore of consciousness. Each child must walk the bridge alone when the time is right. But parents and loved ones can provide handrails on the bridge: we make the journey over feel more peaceful, especially when the bridge wobbles or is quite high. Strong handrails give children the capacity to feel secure so they can look out and enjoy the view. This book aims to support parents in being strong handrails for their children: in being aware of children's development, and in providing reassuring rhytmns of connection along with activities and guidance.

Growing Children, Thriving Children: Raising 7 to 12 year olds with awareness and confidence is divided into three parts. Part One gives background understanding. It describes the physical, social, emotional and cognitive changes of the middle years. This knowledge shows parents the road ahead. The more we can step into our children's shoes, and comprehend what is new or challenging for them, the easier it becomes to offer them understanding and empathy. Knowledge also allows parents to feel prepared, and to respond calmly when change occurs. Recognising what is happening for our children fosters their feeling of being seen, and being unconditionally loved.

As well as describing stages of development, *Growing Children, Thriving Children: Raising 7 to 12 year olds with awareness and confidence* is full of inspiring and practical ideas to help make family life run smoothly and strengthen connection between family members. Many of these are found in Part Two, with helpful tips and activities to inspire family fun and creativity. I also discuss the daily, weekly and yearly rhythms and routines that nourish bonds, even when children no longer want a cuddle before bedtime.

Part Three is for the moments when parents are lost for words – I know how it feels! I share ideas to help with managing children's anger and anxiety, while developing their life skills and fostering greater family harmony. Part Three also provides new creative discipline strategies for children who are growing in independence and becoming more critical in their thinking. I answer common parent questions concerning this age group, offering real-life solutions. Also in Part Three I aim to develop parents' confidence to speak with their children about important puberty topics.

The final chapter looks to the future: it discusses the 12-year transformation, helping parents ease into the teenage years.

This book makes sense read from start to finish, but it is also designed so parents can go straight to the chapter they most need, or they can dip in and out of the different parts.

Each chapter of this book includes the voices of children, as well as insights and stories from parents and teachers. I believe it takes a community to write a practical and insightful book, and I'd like to thank everyone for raising their voices to share and to inspire others.

There is no such thing as perfect parenting: this is not a guide to getting it all right. We all make mistakes and wish we could turn the clock back, myself included! But I believe we can strive to understand the world our children inhabit and how they see it. We can reach for new ideas and we can commit to reconnecting with the young people we love over and over again during the ups and downs of parenting. This kind of striving is a gift for our children. I feel blessed that you have picked up my book and that we are all striving together.

Growing Children, Thriving Children: Raising 7 to 12 year olds with awareness and confidence aims to be a companion for parents. My hope is to increase understanding of the changes during middle childhood, to create a few 'light-bulb' moments for the reader and to provide practical ideas to enhance childrens' lives and to strengthen family bonds. Together we can guide children across the changes at 7, 9 and 12 years with confidence, enjoyment and love.

PART ONE
What to Know

When we are aware of how children view the world (externally) and themselves (internally) at different ages, we understand their development on a deeper level. This helps us respond to changes and challenges with compassion and wisdom, and it can give children the sense of being seen and held while their sense of self, their outlook and their bodies transform.

Part One of *Growing Children, Thriving Children* provides a detailed overview of the 7-year change and the 9-year crossing, explaining children's experience and behaviour, and offering helpful ways for parents and carers to respond to childhood developmental changes in a positive and caring manner.

CHAPTER ONE
The 7-Year Change Explained

The first of the significant transitions of the middle years happens at about age 7 when children are losing their baby teeth. Children's metamorphoses can be compared to caterpillars turning into butterflies and venturing out of their cocoons: there is change on all levels.

In this chapter, I will describe in turn the

* physical,
* social,
* emotional, and
* cognitive

changes your children are likely to experience around the age of 7.

Physical Changes

Parents can watch for these physical changes in their children:

* milk teeth fall out to be replaced with adult teeth,
* faces become longer,
* the round belly of early childhood disappears as the body stretches,
* fingers and limbs elongate.

In fact, after age 7 almost all the cells in the body have been replaced since birth: this really is a different physical body from the newborn child.

> ## Voice of a Parent: Martine
>
> I observed my 7-year-old child the other day with a new awareness: his body is now really long! I also noticed that his face is more refined, and his chin is defined. I began to imagine how he will look as an adult for the first time.

Clumsiness

Getting used to a longer body can take time, and meanwhile there may be an increase in minor accidents: knocking over drinks, for example, or tripping up. Recognising the physical changes in children, seeing the new form of body they are adjusting to, can help us provide a calm and compassionate parental response to clumsiness, rather than reacting in anger. The awkward stage will pass.

Movement games

Movement throughout childhood is vitally important, especially at the age of 7 years. To assist with the grounding of their new bodies, children require wide opportunities for play that involves their whole physical being. They need plenty of time outside in an environment where they can test their spatial orientation skills by balancing, climbing, running and building creative structures, while discovering the world and themselves. This is a great age for riding bikes and scooters.

Movement patterns that incorporate three main regions – above and below the waist, left and right side of the body, and forwards and backwards in motion – help integrate children's midlines and reflexes, which is essential for 7-year-olds' development. Movement games that cross one or more of these midlines include hopscotch and skipping, balancing, ball and beanbag games, clapping and string games. In turn, these gross-motor developments in the body continue to expand neuron connections in the brain. There is also a link between gross-motor movements of the body and fine-motor patterns in the fingers. To form letters, the pencil must make small movements above and below, left and right, forwards and backwards. Coordinated bodies can lead to coordinated handwriting over time.

Chapter 6 of this book, titled 'I'm Bored!', describes some fun gross-motor movement games.

Voice of a 7 Year Old: Saffire

My brother and I play a game in the park: we try and go on all the play equipment without touching the ground. This is our favourite game.

Fine-motor skills and craft

Fine-motor movement with craft and handwork is beneficial for finger dexterity and testing the now lengthy fingers of 7 year olds. They love craft and making things! Knitting is a superb activity, and children in Steiner-Waldorf schools use their longer fingers to play the recorder in Class One. Fine-motor activities also join neurons in the brain. Why do Occupational Therapists provide basket weaving and fine-motor activities for rehabilitation? Because working with the fingertips rewires the brain!

Children aged 7 can wash and dress themselves independently (buttons and zips, but often not shoelaces), although calm reminders might be needed to keep your child on track during the morning routine. At this age there is also increased finger control for chopping food: invite children to assist with meal preparations. Expect a rise in hunger as the body grows – 7 year olds need wholesome, nutritious and satisfying foods as they move through developmental changes.

There are craft ideas and recipes to inspire family cooking in the chapter titled 'I'm Bored!'

Voice of a Teacher: Cathy

I noticed recently how much the Class One children, who all turn 7 this year, love string games, finger rhymes and clapping games. All these activities are so popular in the classroom right now. I also have witnessed an increase in spilt paint and accidents outside.

Social Changes

Before the 7-year change, children's play arises from discovering toys and objects close by: the child sees the block and decides to build a castle tower. After the 7-year change, play begins as an internal process: the child first thinks of making a castle and then goes to find the blocks. Planning and preparing for play now takes more time than play itself. This new style of play often relies on social interaction and teamwork, or time spent pondering ideas alone. Play lasts for longer, is increasingly complex, and one theme or project can last over a period of weeks.

Voice of a Parent: Martine

My twin 7-year-old boys now play for greater periods of time together. There is so much preparation. Their storytelling capacity during play is amazing! They narrate everything that happens during play. The doll's house is a favourite: each room has the furniture carefully planned, and they develop in-depth scripts for the doll characters. They describe family members and what is going on in considerable detail.

Outside, it is all about digging! I watched one of my sons through the window as he worked out an engineering strategy to manoeuvre the wheelbarrow over a fence independently. He wanted to dig in a new area!

Creativity and imaginative play

Children at age 7 are very imaginative and creative. Popular play items include costumes and props for playing roles, miniature play animals and small dolls for storytelling, bricks or blocks for building and constructing, and materials for craft and drawing. At this age, children enjoy fairy tales and magic, and also inventing things. Cardboard boxes can be great for new inventions. Playing outdoors provides opportunities to create sand potions or fairy landscapes.

Tip - Keep Toys!

Don't be in a hurry to get rid of toys or assume that children are too old to play with them. The style of play will change, but the play will continue. The doll's house will now be an intricate part of storytelling, and blocks will be used for architectural designs rather than simple tall towers.

Voice of a Teacher: Cathy

There is the most wonderful 'engineering' play occurring during break times at school. Every day I hear a group of children think aloud and discuss their plans to transform the sandpit. The designs include pipes and tunnels, and they create road-making machines. During the summer, they added a hosepipe and water to their sandpit design. And, to their amazement, frogs came!

Emotional Changes

What emotional changes can be expected with the transitions at around age 7?

Rudolf Steiner describes the etheric body as being like an energy field that surrounds the physical body, providing health and vitality to each person. During the first seven years children have etheric bodies that are joined with the etheric bodies of their main caregivers. They are wrapped in the parents' 'etheric cloak', in their energy field.

At about the same time that baby teeth are pushed out by new adult teeth, children begin to develop their own separate etheric energy field. There is a subtle parting from parents, often noticed particularly by the mother. It is important to recognise that children are becoming aware of their own separateness at a new level.

Testing limits

Parents may hear the words 'You are not the boss of me!' as the etheric connection subtly changes and loosens. Children at 7 often go through patches of testing limits and pushing boundaries. I discuss shifts in discipline strategies that can help decrease emotional outbursts in the chapter titled 'That's Unfair!'

When their behaviour has been challenging, talking quietly after the heat of the moment is a useful tool.

Children this age are often powerfully affected by stories. Seek out books and stories that connect to the discipline challenges you are dealing with, or make them up! Weave into your tale a picture of how actions affect the feelings of others. Through stories we can educate our children's hearts, as well as their minds.

Overwhelming emotions

At age 7, children may be particularly aware of their feelings and perhaps somewhat overwhelmed by them. There may be unexplained tears and, at times, short bursts of anger or anxiety or a new sensitivity to everyday situations as children register new bodily sensations and new levels of complexity in the world around them.

Children aged 7 may feel socially alone at times, or that others do not like them. This is often imagined. Children are so present in the moment, and when this is joined with a new sense of separateness and sensitivity, they can lose the broader perspective on the nature of their friendships overall, and they lack emotional skills when small disagreements arise. Friendship issues are often short-lived. It can help to create a classroom or family ethos that affirms: we look after each other.

Sometimes, a short period of melancholy arises, as 7 year olds unconsciously separate from their parents' etheric cloak, and begin to leave early childhood behind.

Each child experiences the 7-year change in a unique way. Sometimes the emotional changes are very subtle, at other times more obvious. Some children tend to be more withdrawn and some are more outgoing.

Although the 7-year change comes with emotional challenges at times, we can expect that childhood in general is a broadly contented and carefree time. If unhappiness continues or if there seems to be a marked shift from a child's usual manner and tendency, it is important to look for other causes.

Swings in confidence

Children going through the 7-year change often swing from being clingy and sensitive to venturing out boldly into new territory. It is common during times of change for children to regress before stepping forward into new ways of being.

This pattern of regressing in order to then move forward can be compared to the action of pulling back an arrow before launching it with a taut bowstring. Children regress to gather energy and certainty, then leap forward into the new stage of development. Interestingly, children at age 7 love playing with pretend bows and arrows, and with paper airplanes, which are also pulled back to be launched forwards.

During this time of developmental change, children may experience stomach aches and growing pains. If your children say they feel sore, provide hot-water bottles, comfort and love.

At times of physical change and emotional flux, children may not want to go to school. Remember that they are usually fine once they are through the classroom door and have said goodbye to their parents. It is often the anticipation of separation that is hardest.

Parents may feel emotional, too, at this time of change. Each member of the family needs time to adapt to a new stage. It's helpful to acknowledge your own losses, and important to then celebrate – even just quietly to yourself – the new developmental steps you see in your children.

Family rhythms for emotional stability

Children at 7 years require parents and adults to love them in a connected way. They need parents who are engaged and trying to perceive the world through their eyes. Children especially flourish with loving daily rhythms. Strong, predictable patterns for greetings, mealtimes, rest and bedtimes give them a sense of security, a feeling that the world is a place that can be understood and trusted. They thrive on regular moments of love and connection. Overtired children can be very emotional, as can children with an unmet need for adult attention.

Chapter 4, 'Daily Connections', is full of everyday activities to help strengthen bonds between parents and children.

A child can feel the weight of the world one minute but move into enthusiastic play and learning the next. Take upsets and ailments seriously, but not too seriously. Provide a base while also encouraging children to step out, assuring them they will still be holding your hand to start the journey, and that hearts remain connected even when we are physically apart.

Voice of a Parent: Martine

Each child experiences the 7-year change differently. I have one 7-year-old twin who is confident and self-assured. My other son has regressed back to using his name when making requests at times of stress: 'Joshua wants to eat...' instead of 'I want to eat...'. He also wants to play koalas and possums, wrapping himself up in blankets and hanging off my neck for cuddles. He cannot be touched enough.

Voice of a Teacher: Cathy

I have noticed that if one child comes to me during the day to say they have a stomach ache, and I give them loving attention, then another child will automatically say they have a stomach ache too. It is like an unconscious signal to say 'Show me more love!'

Although the children in my class are all happy during the day, I have six children who find Monday mornings difficult, with tears when entering the classroom or leaving the home environment. All the children adjust relatively quickly once they are in the room and the parents leave.

Adult news and themes

Children at age 7 see the world as fundamentally good, and they need to hold on to this conviction to feel safe and to confidently grow and develop. Be careful if 7 year olds access the news, absorb scary themes in movies, or if they overhear difficult adult conversations. I am sometimes told about children at this age experiencing nightmares because they have heard or watched stories of violence or tragedy. Where possible, protect the innocence of children. Adult events can be disturbing because children are old enough to follow the news story, images, or grasp the sense of the conversation but have not yet developed the cognitive and emotional tools to fully understand their own place in relation to distressing events. If children are stressed regarding adult news or themes, or experiencing nightmares or anxiety, reassure them of all the goodness in the world, and create a boundary around the news and around the child using simple, graphic terms.

The feeling stage

Rudolf Steiner explains child development as occurring in seven-year stages, the first seven years being the 'will' or 'body' stage. The second stage of childhood, from age 7 to 14, is often described as the 'feeling' stage. When Steiner characterises this age as 'the feeling stage' he is thinking less of emotions such as anger or anxiety or sadness, and more of powerful sensations such as wonder, beauty and goodness. Such sensations are particularly important for 7-year-old children: we adults can usually remember having a heightened sense of such impressions in our own younger years.

This 'feeling' sense is stimulated with delightful play, craft, time in nature, and tales. And also when new concepts and cognitive lessons are introduced with a feeling of wonderment.

Cognitive Changes

During the first six years of life, the child is on the go most of the time, and life is experienced through the child's strong will to move. The focus is on the growing body. After the 7-year change, movement is still very important, but it is not as constant. Periods of sitting still to focus are easier and more relaxed for children.

After the change of teeth, children acquire a greater power of memory. This helps play activities last a week or more, as children remember the details of their plans. It also enables children to retain a story plot from one day to the next, so they will enjoy chapter books read aloud. They can retain more steps to complete a task, which helps with engagement in lessons.

As children aged 7 are in the 'feeling' stage, they often understand best when there is an element to explanations that connects to sensations of awe and wonder. Intellectual concepts are easier for them to grasp and retain when delivered with imagination pictures. Use stories to teach wherever possible.

Learning numbers and letters

In Steiner-Waldorf schools, teaching of numbers and letters is deepened through a sense of feeling: creative, imaginative pictures and stories are given to match the new concepts and enhance understanding. Learning in this way can be exciting and energising, rather than draining for children.

Voice of a Teacher: Cathy

I introduce all the numbers and letters of the alphabet to my children by weaving each one into a story that I continue each day. The story tells of travellers visiting new lands where they discover a new letter or number on every adventure: a stream may represent the letter 'S' and a mountain, the letter 'M'. The travellers always use a golden rope to find their way. The children's eyes light up each time the travellers discover a new letter or number.

On the first day of school, the children entered the classroom holding onto one long golden ribbon. This ties in with the golden rope described in the story. The children are on a journey of learning and discovery, just like the travellers they are hearing about.

Tip - Make Learning Fun

If you are reinforcing school learning at home, tell creative and enjoyable stories: for example, a story about a farmer planting rows of carrots could help when you are talking about counting. Spot house numbers on letterboxes on a local walk. Trace letters or numbers on each other's backs for a guessing game. By using the world around children and appealing to their imagination, learning can be fun and spontaneous.

Voice of a Parent: Martine

The process of learning letters and numbers in an imaginative way was so alive and wonderful for my children that they started spotting letters in nature. They spotted the letter 'A' made with sticks, and 'S' in the bow of a tree. These hidden nature discoveries were met with much enthusiasm and joy.

Age 8

After the 7-year change, at age 8, children are able to hold increasing information from day to day, while still experiencing pure imagination, joy and wonder in the moment. They enjoy simple jokes, riddles, and tongue-twisters. They love to laugh! It is often a more emotionally settled period. Children grow into their longer bodies and become more confident physically: they have fewer clumsy moments. After the 7-year change, children tend to draw pictures of people that show a figure standing on the ground, with hands and feet, and with a waist and a neck. These differ quite distinctly from the circle and stick drawings of younger children. We can see these more mature drawings as depicting the stage the children themselves are experiencing. Their feet and hands now accomplish greater feats. They stand more firmly on the ground. Look at your 7- and 8-year-old children with amazement!

In Brief: The 7-Year Change Explained

* Watch for physical changes: has the body stretched, and the face become longer? How many teeth has your child lost?
* Provide plenty of opportunities to run, climb, balance and play in the natural environment. Set up games of skipping and hopscotch.
* Practice finger dexterity with crafts and encourage children to help with cooking.
* Watch how play changes: can you hear children making elaborate plans together?
* Hold onto the toys of early childhood; your children will still use them for storytelling and construction and moments of stepping back to younger games.
* 7 year olds can test boundaries. After the event, explain how their actions affected others. Use a simple story.
* Connect as a family and create a secure daily rhythm by sharing meals, and by providing comfort and loving touch at bedtime.
* Be prepared for occasional strong emotions, and stomach aches. Provide love and a hot-water bottle.

* Are your children asking a lot of questions? 'What a wonderful question...' is a good response. Try to answer in a manner that is simple and pictorial. Too many dry facts and young eyes tend to glaze over.
* Children love imaginative stories. Weave counting and learning letters into tales.

CHAPTER TWO

Understanding the 9-Year Crossing

The 7-year change and the more settled patch at age 8 are followed by a further major transition at about the age of 9. This nine-year metamorphosis is central to Rudolf Steiner's concept of the Rubicon, and is perhaps the most defining change in this period of development. As mentioned in the Introduction, there is a particular phrase, 'the crossing', that is used to refer to the shift from early childhood to middle childhood – the transformation that usually occurs between the ages of 8½ and 10.

In this chapter, I will explore how three special gifts of early childhood transform with the Rubicon-crossing. If we grasp the special characteristics of early childhood, we will better understand the changes being made by 9 year olds: we will be able to see what is lost and gained in the crossing.

First Gift: The Present Moment

The present moment is the first gift of early childhood. Young children live in the here and now. This really is a 'present'! Their focus is on existing time and immediate reality, not contemplating the future or revisiting the past. Young children are fully engaged in each moment, which explains why they often easily forget a seemingly simple request, for example to get their coat or shoes. If they pass a toy on the way to the shoe or coat rack, play may begin, and the task is forgotten. This isn't really the child's fault! Try spending some time completely in the present moment, with no fear of the future or regrets from the past. It can be a very enlightening experience for adults!

At approximately 9 years of age, the gift of the 'present moment' is left in the kingdom of early childhood. In the new land of middle childhood, the concept of time is experienced differently. It is now observed as a perpetual stream, in which awareness of future events emerge and memories of the past take shape in the present moment. With this new perception of continuous time, children have a greater understanding of the mortality of human life: that one day everybody will die, including their parents.

The death of parents may suddenly become a concern for 9-year-old children. 'Who will look after me if you die?' is a common question, and there may be periods of anxiety in which children may fear future events or hold on to past actions. This can appear to be a backwards step from the confident 8-year-old, but it is a normal part of 'the crossing' for some children. Simple reassurance and comfort from parents and care-givers is the best solution to these concerns.

Chapter 8, 'Suggestions for Anxiety', discusses in more detail how to deal with childhood fears.

Voice of a Teacher: Natalie

When teaching Class Three, I supported a 9-year-old girl through extreme anxiety. She began to cry each day before the home-time bell, but she was never able to tell me why she was crying at the time. Every day after the bell, I would take her hand and squeeze it tightly in a rhythmical motion while reminding her to breathe, particularly accentuating the out-breath, and we would walk down the corridor to the play area, doing this all the way. She required support; her anxiety was real and very distressing until she saw her mother waiting to collect her.

A couple of months later her parents decided to separate; she was obviously feeling sad and overwhelmed.

A few weeks later another girl started to become very nervous that her mother wouldn't be there to pick her up after school. Her mother had to go away for work and had told her a few months before. Her grandfather was also sick and in hospital at the time. I used the same process and would walk down the corridor holding both girls' hands. They soon began to support each other, and by the end of the school year, both girls were much less anxious.

Telling the time

In the Steiner-Waldorf curriculum, telling the time is taught during the 9-year crossing stage of child development. This is the moment of childhood when the notion of clocks and watches, and all aspects of minutes, seconds and hours are easily absorbed. Turning 9 is a good age for buying children their first watch.

Voice of the Author: Lou

I remember sitting in the car with my older sister; I was about 9 years old. It was a journey from the strawberry fields to home, about ten minutes in duration. My sister explained the clock face to me, as I had recently been given a watch. I could tell the time before we reached home. It was like magic! I had instantly grasped all the elements of the watch. It was literally the right 'time' to learn.

Easier daily transitions

Once children understand the concept of time, daily transitions and the routines of family life can become smoother. This is an obvious gain from the 9-year crossing and the loss of living in the present moment. There is now an increased awareness of the bigger picture: children begin to see the temporal structure of when daily and weekly events will occur, as well as grasping school times and the schedule of outings. When children are younger, transition times can be difficult for them to understand due to their involvement in play, whereas older children can look at the clock and keep their own check on time. After the 9-year crossing, future events can also be planned and discussed as a family with greater ease. However, with this new-found consciousness of daily coming and goings, being late may now become of greater concern for children.

When my son was around 9 years old and I was slow to take him out, he pretended to light my 'space rocket engines' to remind me to move quickly – copying a game I had played with him as a child! Though it is worth noting that while all children develop a new perception of time, some still do not mind being late!

Second Gift: Pure Imagination

Early childhood is the only stage of life where 'pure' imagination is experienced. This is the second gift. When a child plays with a wooden block it is transformed into a castle wall, or perhaps a boat. Throughout our lives we are able to be imaginative and creative, but in the back of our minds we know we are pretending that a block of wood is something else. For a young child, the block is no longer a block, it is absolutely a sailing boat on a cloth sea!

During the early years, young children fully take on the role of nurse or doctor while giving remedies to teddies. As they pass through to middle childhood (around 9 or 10 years), they understand that they are pretending, and pure imaginative play becomes progressively more forced.

I have heard of 11 year olds who still ride imaginary horses to school, but they tend to live in less urban and slower-paced environments. The gift of pure imagination can last longer for some children, or ends earlier for others who live in fast-paced, highly technological environments with no creative space and time to play.

Children's play at 9 years

Children at age 9 can appear to play; however, on closer observation, their 'play' is becoming more strategic, with an emphasis on planning, designing, creating, building and construction rather than pure imagination. Lego can be a big hit at this age. Creativity develops, and designing and making doll's clothes, building things from clay or modelling wax, and playing games involving more complex or mechanical thinking are all popular activities for 9-year olds.

Remember – don't get rid of toys too soon. Dolls are required for making doll's clothes, and the sandpit is now used to create magic potions. 9 year olds still love the idea of spells and magic, even if they no longer totally believe it's real.

If 9-year-old children have younger siblings, they are more likely to still play and to set up imaginative games. The role of the older child often becomes more protective, with an emphasis on leading games and play.

Voice of a 9 Year Old: Shaan

I play with my brother and sister, aged 4 and 7. We mostly pretend to cook outside.

My favourite thing to do at home by myself is to think. I really enjoy thinking. I mostly think about different kinds of machines. I have built a robot, a truck that carries blocks and a crane. I don't have to actually build what I'm thinking about. I just like to think.

Voice of a Parent: Lisa

My 9-year-old daughter enjoys creating dolls' clothes. Recently, she took her doll to show and tell at school to display her handiwork. Unfortunately, she was teased for still playing with dolls, but thankfully she has continued to create doll's clothes at home.

Reading, cooking and musical instruments

During middle childhood the act of reading can flourish, and books are often met with enthusiasm, especially if a child is not overstimulated by electronic devices. Without imaginative play, there are many hours to fill, and children enjoy visualizing a story's plot and characters.

Children aged 9 also like to follow recipes and to start to cook meals or bake independently, so put your feet up while the meal is being made!

Learning a musical instrument may be of interest at this time, and in Steiner-Waldorf schools every student begins to play a string musical instrument at 9. Once the impulse to play imaginatively decreases, there may be more time to practise.

A whole day is a long time to fill when pure imagination leaves during middle childhood. It may be tempting to allow for an increase in technology, but then children may miss out on reading and cooking, as well as music, craft and movement activities, all of which can help with developing key practical, creative, physical and cognitive skills.

Voice of a 9 Year Old: Ilija

I love to go outside and build things with mud. At the end of my driveway it is really muddy. Once I carved it all out and made a big town, but it washed away with the rain.

I like to read too. I have read *Tintin*, the *Famous Five* series, and *The Chronicles of Narnia*. I have also read a whole stack of Roald Dahls.

Third Gift: Rose-coloured Glasses

The final gift of early childhood is to experience the world as fundamentally good, with an outlook of wonder, openness and purity.

I heard a story recently of a 4-year-old boy going through a security search entering a sports ground. The guard put his arms out wide to demonstrate how the boy should stand so his torso could be patted down to check for hard objects. But the boy saw the wide arms, and gave the guard a hug! This is how he interpreted the situation – and it's a classically 4-year-old way of seeing.

Young children wear rose-coloured glasses, not taking in the duality in the world of good and bad. It is a wonderfully innocent stage. Traditional fairy tales and other appropriate stories for young children may depict challenges, but the endings are harmonious – goodness always prevails. Young children also believe in all kinds of happy magic: Father Christmas, the tooth fairy and the Easter bunny are all seen as completely realistic concepts; logical thinking has not yet awoken. Young children accept these magical characters as the way the world works. They believe wholeheartedly in wonder! And it is important that they do.

During the 9-year-old crossing the rose-coloured glasses are taken off; the veil is lifted, and children begin to see the world in a more practical and logical manner. They have a growing realisation that people and scenarios are in fact not always good, and this can create a subtle internal disturbance in children, including increased anxiety and fear.

It is common for a 9-year-old child to look under the bed before bedtime or suddenly run fast as if someone is chasing them. They may anticipate an imagined danger. Children at 9 may become afraid of the dark or sleeping alone. This is often brought on by their growing awareness of this duality of light and dark in the world. They may ask for a permanent night-light or to sleep close to other people.

When my own children were young, I brought the camping mattress out of the shed and left it against the wall in our bedroom. The children knew if they were scared that they could sleep there. This worked: they came in periodically during the middle years, and were able to gain comfort from our closeness without waking us up.

Voice of a 9 Year Old: Ilija

At night I like a night-light on and the door left open. I like to hear my mum and dad's voices in other rooms. I'm frightened of fear itself, I don't want to be frightened. I don't like the feeling of being shocked.

Guidelines for 'good' living

At age 9, children enjoy rules for 'good' living and fairness. Guidelines provide a framework for them to live inside, allowing them to feel safe, protected and secure during times of transformation.

The Steiner-Waldorf Class Three school curriculum for 9 year olds includes the topic of the Ten Commandments. This may be a puzzling theme for parents who presume it to be a religious ethos; however, familiarity with the Ten Commandments can be reassuring for children at this stage of their development. The topic conveys the idea that rules for 'good' living exist. There is a certainty to this Biblical account of what is right that is helpful when children are confronting their own uncertainty regarding good and bad in the world. Systems of right living from other faiths and cultures can evoke the same feeling.

This new inclination for rules and guidelines can be useful! I have seen some classes write their own classroom rules for happier days and respectful interaction. Some families create and write down their own guiding ideas for living together more harmoniously.

You may notice that your 9 year old feels very strongly about actions that appear strange, unhealthy or unsafe to them, for example if a family member smokes.

Voice of a Teacher: Natalie

Children can become fascinated with playing out 'good' and 'evil' in the world in order to understand this duality in life. I remember my whole class of 9 year olds playing cops and robbers in the playground. The robbers would be sent to prison, while the cops would work together to capture them.

Goodness in the world

As with 7 year olds, children during middle childhood still require limits to witnessing and hearing news stories of disasters, crime or war. Even though they are becoming more realistic about the world, adult themes are best left until well after the 12-year transformation. Sudden exposure may create a period of melancholy and fear.

With this new awareness of the realities and duality of life, it is all the more important to encourage wonder and a recognition of goodness in children of this age. Share stories of kindness in the world, point out people who have been compassionate, and acknowledge the kind and loving qualities of others. Try to promote the message that although there is good and bad, we can focus on growing 'light', and let our hearts guide us. When children realise that they can see goodness in others, they may become less fearful of the world around them.

Voice of a Parent: Lisa

Within the first half hour after putting my son to bed, he often comes to me to share a nightmare. I now realise that he thinks and worries about aspects of life as he goes to sleep, or the act of sleep is like a death, and he feels disturbed with this more conscious sensation. We've now started playing a gratitude game in the evening to change his mindset before falling asleep.

Holding Hands with Your Children Through the 9-year Crossing

Going through the crossing in middle childhood may appear to be easy for some children but be an intense time for others. Let the individual child lead the way and try not to push children into new stages of awareness too early or hold them back. The crossing has to take place for every child at some point: we all leave early childhood behind. It is often a subtle experience and therefore requires a subtle response from parents. There is no need to talk about or intellectualise this concept with children.

The loss of the three gifts of early childhood may appear a sad idea to parents at first, but remember that children take the nurture, wonder and imagination of early childhood into their future. Rudolf Steiner said that what children receive at 2 years, we see in their development at 22. In this sense, nothing is truly lost.

And there is so much to enjoy at this stage of family life. With their new awareness of time, children like to be part of the planning process for family activities, to be included in formulating holidays, outings, events, choices for meal plans and more. Children of this age also grasp the concept of winning and losing more fully, perceiving future wins, so losses are not so dramatic. This means now is the perfect time for family board games! And with more time on their hands without imaginative play, their interest in helping around the home may grow: for example, they may enjoy assisting with cooking, gardening and caring for pets.

The ideas in this chapter paint a picture of how 9-year-old children experience the world. In the next chapter we will discover how 9 year olds experience themselves.

In Brief: Understanding the 9-Year Crossing

* How does your child experience time? Consider whether they are pondering the future and past more often now. Does your child own a watch or clock?
* Observe children during their free time. How do they fill their hours?
* Which books interest your children? See Chapter 6, 'I'm Bored!' for reading recommendations.
* Do your children have opportunities to cook at home?
* Do they have any creative projects or building plans underway?
* Are you aware of any fears your child has? Night-lights are common sleeping aids for 9 year olds.
* Speak to your children of the goodness in the world. Share a gratitude game every day.
* Board games are fun now. What are your family favourites?
* Remember the crossing is subtle and requires a subtle response. Each child has a different experience. Observe your child and try to step into their shoes.

CHAPTER THREE
Transformation Time at 9

We have discovered the shifts in how children perceive the world around them before and after the 9-year crossing. In this chapter we will examine how children experience themselves during this transitional time: in other words, the important changes that happen from within.

Inner Changes

The main impulse during early childhood is that of imitation. Children imitate others to make sense of the world. In a significant change that occurs during the 9-year crossing, the impulse to imitate declines. Children start to see themselves as separate from their parents and other children, in fact isolated from the world around them, and therefore they develop a new special relationship to 'self'.

Between the ninth and tenth years... a child gradually awakens to the difference between self and the surrounding world. Only then does a child become aware of being a separate 'I'.

RUDOLF STEINER, *THE CHILD'S CHANGING CONSCIOUSNESS,* LECTURE 5.

> ## Voice of a Teacher: Natalie
>
> After the 9-year crossing, the class begins to sing in rounds. During Class Four, small groups of children sing different song parts at the same time. At this age, children can retain their tune and words, even while others close by are singing differently. This is a picture of the child discovering their separate self from others, and holding their own ground – and also their own note!

Powerful milestones

Before the age of 2½ to 3 years, young children refer to themselves by their name, for example, 'Johnny would like a drink' or 'Johnny wants the ball'. It is a profound moment (perhaps around age 3) when young children start to refer to themselves as 'I' for the first time: 'I'd like a drink', 'I'd like my bike, please'. This milestone indicates a first awakening of being separate from others. This is the first birth of the 'I' and represents a time of 'I can…'.

The power of the separate self then has a new awakening during the 9-year crossing. The child before 9 felt at one with the world, with beauty, wonder and goodness. After the crossing, children have a realisation that they are in fact separate from others and the world around them, and that they are a unique person. The second birth of the 'I', around 9, signifies a realisation that 'I am alone'.

Am I adopted?

Inquisitive questions about links and background are typical when children discover their uniqueness within the family. 'Who do I look like, Mum or Dad?' And even 'Are you sure I am not adopted?' This is a common thought for a 9 year old: with their new sense of uniqueness and separateness, they wonder if they belong.

Representing a sense of change

It is common at this age for children to ask to be called by a different name to their nickname of earlier childhood, or what they perceive to be a 'baby' name. Instead of 'Jessie', my daughter asked to be called 'Jess'. It is also usual for children to request a bedroom revamp after the 9-year crossing: to get rid of the pictures and rows of teddies now perceived as childish and replace them with a more mature look.

Physical Changes

Watch and wait, the 9-year body goes through a further transformation beyond the 7-year change: a growth spurt leading to increased height, and more defined facial features.

Have you ever watched children with awe: cartwheeling across the grass, swinging upside down on the monkey bars? You are most likely watching a 9-year-old child. There is a fascination at this age with challenging gravity and testing physical boundaries. In a nutshell, children of this age feel more grounded in their body and on the earth. Days are filled with practising physical skills: riding scooters, enjoying longer bike rides and perfecting the handstand. Time can be taken to master a skill by repeating it over and over again, whether kicking a ball or trying a backflip on the trampoline. At 10 years old, girls' bodies grow at a faster rate than boys', but in most children the occasional clumsiness of the 7-year-old child is replaced with a more agile and co-ordinated 9 year old.

Voice of a Parent: Carole

After my son turned 9, I dreamt that he slid down an enormous slide to the ground. It was like he had landed on earth. Around the same time, I noticed two changes: he was able to sit on a chair for long periods, whereas in the past he was always falling off, and he widened his palate of food choices. He literally seemed more grounded on the earth.

Social Changes

We have covered how 9 year olds test their physical boundaries, but how does the 9-year crossing affect their relationships with parents and peers?

Testing boundaries

Young children tend to look up to parents and teachers. Adults are natural authority figures for them. After the crossing, parents and teachers will need to *earn* respect from children. Children aged 9 want to be assured that decisions are fair and reasonable: do their parents *really* know best?

There is no better time to become conscious in your own thoughts and actions than when you are parenting a 9 year old. You will be questioned and scrutinised for integrity, authenticity, wisdom and truth. Children in their middle years will not follow orders to 'Do as I say' if what is asked feels unfair or unjust to them.

You can find suggestions for effective and positive discipline, in addition to discussions of common challenges, in Part Three of this book.

After the crossing, children can manage growing independence in some aspects of self-care, for example teeth cleaning and general cleanliness, although you may find they avoid showers and baths. A teenager will begin to shower every day to avoid being smelly, but a middle-years child is too involved with life and their activities to care. Don't worry about it too much: before the teen years, children don't need to wash so often anyway. Washing avoidance will naturally change as they grow, so save your breath now!

Voice of a Parent: Lisa

I have just realised that my 11-year-old son locks the bathroom door and runs the shower while sitting and reading his book. He doesn't even get wet! It is all a pretence when I ask him to shower each morning.

Lou explained that this kind of mischievousness is a sign of growing independence and sense of self, and said my son was totally absorbed in the next part of his book. Testing boundaries occasionally is a normal stage of child development. She suggested we play a radio in the bathroom during shower time to make it more interesting, and that has helped.

Challenging moments

After their Rubicon changes, 9-year-old children see their parents without rose-coloured glasses. I often joke in my Conscious Parenting classes that parents should sing to young children even if they are out of tune, as the child will not notice until they are 9! At this age, children develop increased awareness, and with this comes comparisons, and a leap in critical thinking and judgement. I often hear parents say, 'My child is 9 years old, going on 14!' This sudden teenage attitude can be a shock for parents, but while there may be moments of defiance and strong moods, this adjustment in perception will settle down, especially if we as parents adjust our perceptions too. We have the task of letting go of our early-years children and starting to see our young people in a new light.

There are still a few more years to go before the teenage years, and children during middle childhood continue to enjoy cuddles and family activities, and to spend time outside of their bedrooms in the shared rooms of the house. It is important to build loving connections into family life through daily conversations and shared experiences, making time to talk about qualities of kindness, trust and honesty, which will raise children up to noble acts while they are in the feeling stage and open to a sense of nobility and rightness.

It is not uncommon for children to leave home for a secluded place in the garden or to sit at the end of the driveway because a decision appears unfair. With this new awareness of fairness, matched with a growing sense of self and independence, they may head out of the door with a snack in their pocket. It won't be long before they come back, realising it is not that much fun in the world alone.

Voice of a Parent: Lisa

My daughter was very upset due to feeling that life was unfair at home, so she packed her suitcase to live in her tree house. It was summer, and we live on a large rural property, so she was safe. She ventured up the tree with her suitcase, and came down not long afterwards, missing the family mealtime and her own bed, and realising that she was loved.

Self-criticism

This new tendency to make comparisons and judgements can be internalised too, and children now begin to compare themselves with others. The 'inner critic' appears, and parents may hear children repeat 'I'm not good enough...' At such moments, parents and caregivers can reinforce the idea that every child has a gift to share with the world and something to learn and practise. Everyone is a wonderful individual; no one is exactly the same.

With growing self-awareness, a desire for a certain 'look' may start surprisingly young. Around 9 years of age I asked my dad a question:

'Am I pretty?' His answer was perfect. He took some time to ponder before replying, 'I think you are attractive, you have a big smile, warm heart, and one day someone will love you for who you truly are. You may be my daughter, but I enjoy being with you as a person.' Well, I was on cloud nine! I thought being attractive was way better than being pretty!

Social changes with peers

With this new special relationship to self, it is natural for 9 year olds to subtly move away from their parents or closest caregivers. Children may now look to their peers, and you might hear lots of stories being shared at home, for example 'Jennifer thinks...' or 'At school, John said...'

The middle years are also a time when deeper friendships based on loyalty and shared interests develop. Age 9 can be a good time to start sleepovers at a friend's house and is often the age for the first residential class camp away from home.

Friendships are important at this age. If friendships are tumultuous, children can feel alone. Creating family rhythms of connections, card and board games, and regular outings help children to look forward to events and to feel that they belong despite what is happening among their friends. If children feel socially isolated, perhaps widen their circle of friends – create social gatherings with nieces and nephews, neighbourhood pals or family friends.

Emotional Changes

Is your child moody, assertive, angry one minute and cuddly the next? Stay calm; with the powerful 'I' emerging as they leave early childhood, heated emotions may spill over. Increased frustration with parents' decisions and a new feeling of self-consciousness and isolation may lead to emotional outbursts from time to time. Have compassion and don't take the moods of a 9 year old to heart.

Their growing sense of aloneness can lead to melancholy moments and fearful tendencies. It is common for children at this age to experience unpredictable mood swings, one moment happy, the next grumpy. This can shock both children themselves, and their parents. With some children, anxiety and fear may increase, fuelled by an unconscious uncertainty of the world. Other emotions may include restlessness, clinginess, withdrawal and sadness. These are not a backwards step; they are part of the journey to new developmental shores. Emotions may create headaches, stomach aches, and physical dizziness.

The first chapters of Part Three in this book are specifically about anger and anxiety, and you will find more tools there to overcome fears and furies.

Life skills

With all these inner changes, developing life skills will foster feelings of safety for children and help to settle emotions. Cooking may become a favourite pursuit. Cubby- and den-building is often a popular activity. Similarly, learning to pitch tents, camping and gathering firewood all speak to children on a far deeper level than meets the eye. The underlying feeling is 'I'm alone in this world but I can feed myself and build a shelter'.

The Class Three Steiner-Waldorf school curriculum includes a number of life skills activities:

*   growing wheat to then grind and make bread
*   jam-making
*   building projects, such as designing and creating model houses (small scale), or making mud bricks to create a building (large scale)
*   knitting and crocheting an item of clothing, e.g. a scarf, hat, or poncho

Such activities follow the lead of the children and reassure them that even though they may feel separate on an unconscious level, they have the skills to care for themselves. Completing projects like this at home also provides the chance to learn together: make a family recipe book or find out how to knit a scarf!

Voice of a Teen: Gabi

I remember when I was about 9 years of age, we learnt all about money at school. First, we made islands. I was with Annabel and we made things out of beeswax, then we traded goods with other islands.

Cognitive Changes and the Development of Memory

Children's capacity to retain information improves with the stronger development of their memory. A 9 year old can be interrupted for a period and then come back to the topic at hand. At home you might observe that your middle-years child likes to see the whole picture to start with, then plans the steps needed to accomplish a goal. Children are developing new cognitive abilities to focus for longer periods and to follow instructions.

In the previous chapter we discovered that the time is now ripe for understanding the clock. Similarly, the Steiner-Waldorf maths curriculum covers measurement and money at this age. The skill of measurement is put into practice to build houses and follow recipes. Monetary knowledge is necessary for living in the world and is easily absorbed by 9 year olds.

Trading games and money

Observe children and you'll see that 9 and 10 year olds naturally play trading games. Swapping sport team cards is a very popular activity at this age, along with stickers. My daughter's class all created sticker books, and every day they traded with each other with great excitement. A parent recently shared with me how her son lined his miniature cars up in order of value for a trading game. Children also like to collect things, such as stamps or coins.

Money is very exciting to this age group! After the crossing, my daughter started to breed guinea pigs to sell. Children aged 9 and 10 like to do extra jobs for pocket money. Giving your child a few coins in exchange for a special household project, beyond normal everyday chores, can help develop their sense of purpose and responsibility. The topic of chores is covered in the chapter answering common parent questions.

Is Father Christmas Real?

Have you noticed that the average age for a child to ask if Father Christmas is real is around the age of 9 or 10 years? Can someone really travel across the whole world in one night pulled through the sky by reindeer? As cognitive abilities develop, so does logical thinking. As children get older, these stories become increasingly questionable. How do we as parents authentically answer this question?

It is a rite of passage for children to enquire whether Father Christmas is real. This shows a new stage of development is underway: they are leaving the dream-like magic of early childhood behind.

A good response is always: 'What do you think?' This question can give us some awareness of the child's perspective. If children are young, and have a continuing desire to believe, but have they have been influenced by another child or sibling, a reasonable answer is, 'If you believe in him, then he is real.'

When children question this logic and move beyond the magical stage of early childhood, a good response may be something along the lines of 'Father Christmas is real in that he is based on St Nicholas, who loved childhood and all children. At Christmas time we celebrate this love for childhood and all children everywhere.'

It is good to remind children that they are now 'protectors' of the Christmas magic for younger children, and that they can help to be Father Christmas too. For example, ask them to help wrap the presents, or suggest buying or making a surprise gift for a neighbour to leave on their doorstep to spread kindness.

Voice of a Parent: Kaz

I vividly remember being around 10 years old when I was determined to stay awake to see Father Christmas. I managed to keep my eyes open, only to see my dad sneak in with my presents. I remember thinking, 'Wow! It has been my dad all along.' With this thought came an appreciation of all that my parents did for me.

The golden years

If you have a sense of sadness as your children lose beliefs in, for example, Father Christmas, it can help to know that the 10th and 11th years of childhood are sometimes referred to as the 'golden years'. This time is the heart of childhood, halfway to 21. Physically, children can be very beautiful and graceful. During Class Five in Steiner-Waldorf schools, children hold their own Greek Olympics. The focus is not on winning, but on style, grace and balance.

During these golden years, emotions can become more balanced, new concepts are readily absorbed, beliefs about the environment and nature are strong, and children enjoy being part of a family team.

Crossing Back and Forth

It is important to state that there is no fixed age for the Rubicon Crossing. It may happen as early as 8½ and as late as 11, although 9½ is the average age. It is also normal to cross back and forth for a while, to swing between the two worlds of being tactile and imaginative and then a little more distant and refusing 'baby' things.

The 9-year crossing will be experienced in different ways by different children. However, with leaving early childhood behind, there are two resounding unspoken questions for every child: 'Do you still love me?' and 'Do you accept me as who I am?'

Family routines and rituals help children feel this love and acceptance every day, and in the next chapter I will discuss ways of utilising these rhythms to improve daily connectivity with your child, reinforcing feelings of love and stability during this period of change and for the future.

In Brief: Transformation Time at 9

* Has your child asked to be called a different name or for a change of bedroom decor? Wait for their lead ...
* Observe your child's physical body. Is it changing? Are they practising a new skill?
* Decisions need to be fair and make sense.
* Self-care skills are blossoming – but your child may not like to shower!

* Leaving early childhood behind may create occasional mood swings. Stay aware and remain calm.
* Include opportunities to develop life skills in a fun way; invite your 9 year old to cook with you.
* Does your child have an interest in trading or collecting anything?
* With a new knowledge of money, children like to complete extra chores or create a lemonade to sell drinks to neighbours.
* Every child is different, and experiences developmental changes in a unique way and time. Observe…
* Love will lead the way. As children change, there is a deep yet subtle desire to feel loved and accepted.

PART TWO
What to Do

During the middle years of childhood, we can be surprised when children are no longer interested in their usual playful routines at bedtime nor in their former choices for imaginative play.

During these years, it is important for families to reconnect on a new level, and also to foster leisure activities that encourage movement and creative thinking. Part Two is full of practical suggestions for easily and simply incorporating loving togetherness into each day. It also has fun ideas for active, creative things to do.

CHAPTER FOUR
Daily Connections

As explained in Part One, by definition growing up is unstable in nature because children's perceptions of the world change, and they are discovering their own sense of personal identity. While children are experiencing these inner changes, they need us to provide outer stability in the form of predictable daily rhythms of connection and communication.

We can call regular daily household activities and routines 'family rhythms', as they create the steady beat underlying the inevitable ups and downs of life. These daily rhythms are at the core of human experience. At a very basic level we all wake up in the morning, eat, work/play/ study, have an evening meal, rest and sleep. Every family has its own unique way of maintaining these daily activities, influenced by culture, location, and parents' work and wider lives.

While these daily rhythms and routines may appear mundane, they are, in fact, sacred. They are the means by which we strengthen our personal family connections, and they are the foundation for human nourishment – physical, mental, emotional, social and spiritual.

All children – all humans – need to belong. We are not meant to live in isolation. Daily family rhythms and routines provide the glue to secure this integral sense of belonging and connection, to cultivate close bonds now and into the future.

As children outgrow sitting on laps, holding hands, maybe even bedtime cuddles, which activities continue to foster connection between you and your children? Eating evening meals together and talking about your day. A bedtime whisper of loving words. Family games night. Driving and chatting on the way to a regular sporting activity, perhaps? Every family has their own regular times to connect together. It is vital that we recognise how important these are during middle childhood as our children step forward into new stages of development, they require positive rhytmns of connction, love and stability.

Family Rhythms in Middle Childhood

At times, the busyness of life can take over. Every day is full of school runs, work, digital distractions and other activities. It can feel like there is no time to really connect with our children, especially as the bonds of early childhood begin to loosen. But this is not the time to disconnect. Middle childhood provides an opportunity to reinforce bonds in new ways through family rhythms that suit your children's stage of development.

Rudolf Steiner explained child development using seven-year cycles. The first seven years of life represent 'body' awareness, with touch and movement being important foundation aspects to early childhood. During the next seven years, from ages 7 to 14, the sense of 'feeling' is prominent. During this stage, conversations will take over from touch to some degree to strengthen feelings of connection and love between parents and children.

This chapter aims to provide practical guidance in establishing and maintaining daily family rhythms that allow conversation and connection, even when parents feel time-poor, stretched or, at times, rejected. The following ideas can foster feelings of security, inclusion, connection, love and joy during the middle years of childhood.

Morning Rhythms

Mornings can sometimes feel like a rush to get everyone out of the door on time, but it's important that children are met with a moment of warmth to start the day, like the rising of the sun.

Loving words

Loving words begin the day in a positive way. As a morning greeting, I would simply say 'My love' or 'My beautiful' with a quick embrace. Dedicate a few seconds each morning to displaying love, rather than a growl to get ready!

One way for parents to bring more warmth into the family day is to think of words and actions as pebbles. Imagine starting each day with ten pebbles in one pocket. With each expression of warmth and love to a child, move one pebble across to the imaginary pocket on the other side, starting with a positive morning greeting. Each evening, think back over your interactions with your child that day. Did all ten pebbles travel across?

Tip - Three Squeezes for 'I Love You'

I was recently listening to American talk show host Jimmy Fallon speak about his late mother. He explained that they had played a special hand-squeezing game together. Three squeezes meant 'I love you'. This could easily be used as a morning greeting, or at the school gate as a subtle farewell.

Voice of a Parent: Azin

We play a 'gratitude' game in the car on the way to school every morning. Each person thinks of three things to be grateful for. This daily ritual creates a magic moment for my children and starts the day in a positive way.

Rest Rhythms

Instead of returning home from school and work to busyness and disconnection, try creating a twenty-minute rest time for everyone, parents included, and make this part of your daily rhythm. This can create a more relaxed pre-dinner atmosphere. Each day is made up of 'breathing in' and 'breathing out' moments: school is 'breathing out' time, with structured learning, social interactions, and physical activity. Once home, 'breathing in' keeps family life in harmony and balance.

The following suggestions are examples of twenty-minute after-school connection activities, but they will work any time 'breathing-in' together is required.

Reading together

After school, children's (and parents') moods may be negatively influenced by hunger and tiredness – also known as being 'hangry'! Prepare a quick afternoon snack of chopped fruit and vegetables, and a drink while your child finds their current chapter book. The power of reading to children is not to be underestimated. On a physical level, their breathing will slow and deepen, and the body will gradually unwind and become more relaxed. A parent's voice allows children to go into an almost hypnotic, subconscious state, allowing them to imagine mental pictures, connect to characters and unconsciously absorb moral issues. This develops their creative capacities, and expands their impressions of life, and so much more… The open, relaxed feeling of reading aloud and listening also allows any issues that have occurred during the day to melt away or arise for discussion. It creates an opportunity for connection. The book you read might also inspire discussions or questions, which can provide some interesting topics of conversation for dinner time later on.

Classic chapter books are perfect for 7 to 10 year olds. Chapter 6, 'I'm Bored!', includes a list of recommended books to read together during the middle years.

If there is no time after school to share a chapter book, bedtime is another great moment for reading together.

Voice of a Teen: Jess

Mum read to me after school each day. If the day was really hot, she would shut all the curtains and read to me. I remember it being very relaxing, especially when I was tired. When I have to read an uninteresting book now, Mum occasionally reads it to me.

Resting together

Even spending as little as ten minutes after school to 'breathe in' and rest can be nurturing for both parents and children. Take time for a quiet chat on the sofa, or perhaps a nurturing game.

My daughter was 7 when I found two identical foot spas in the local second-hand shop. I would add a few drops of lavender to the water, and while I read a chapter book aloud, we would soak our feet together. It wasn't long before my son's toes ventured in too!

Tip - Home-made Foot Spa

You can create a foot spa easily at home by filling a washing-up bowl with warm water and a few drops of essential oil. Place marbles on the bottom. Now roll your feet for pure relaxation!

Voice of a Parent: Jenny

When my children and I arrive home after a busy school day, we head straight to my big bed for a rest. My children join me to chat, and to read stories. I love this half an hour together. Afterwards I feel ready to prepare the evening meal, sometimes with my children's help.

Cooking together

The demands of modern family life mean that the evening meal is often prepared in a rush. If there is no opportunity for a restful twenty minutes after school, a parent and child cooking together can create the same feeling of connection and communication. Asking children to join in with simple food preparation establishes ownership and appreciation of the meal, as well as being a way for them to contribute to the family. It also teaches important practical life skills. If children do not wish to join in, there is always another day, although parents should be aware that children are more likely to want to help if they are not plugged into screen-based technology straight after school.

If you find that you regularly get home too late to cook together, try preparing the evening meal in the morning, or cook dishes together over the weekend and freeze meals for the week ahead.

Voice of a Parent: Chloe

After school I'm often in the kitchen, and my children ask to help, or I encourage them to join me. I find that while cooking together we chat and connect. Once the meal is made, they receive thanks for their help and cooking capabilities, which is good for their caring skills too.

Chatting together

Daily communication times form a strong foundation in middle childhood, which is important for the upcoming teenage years. Children need to feel that they can talk to their parents, and that there are always opportunities for communication.

If your child does not want to connect or chat, try not to be offended. Develop a playful attitude. Silence is good too. Different children have different temperaments: some are chatty and outgoing, others are reserved and quiet. Watch for cues from children, observe and be emotionally available. The biggest present children receive is our 'presence', so make sure your child knows you're available if they want to talk. Place phones in a basket up high during daily connection times. Putting your own phone away implicitly says to children: 'This moment is important for me, and so are you!'

Children may be more open to chatting when not giving direct eye contact, so the journey home from school (in the car or walking) and resting activities can provide good opportunities for daily connection.

Voice of a Parent: Peter

In the car home from school, I ask my two children, 'How was your day?' The one-word answer is always, 'Good'. I then say, 'Tell me one thing that was good?' And off they go…

Mealtime Rhythms

The dinner table is a place to build the family 'tribe' during middle childhood, to cultivate a feeling of belonging together. Ask children to set the table so they feel part of the preparation. A candle and vase of flowers can make the space feel special. Turning off all phones and tablets and the TV indicates that mealtimes are important. Their importance lies not only in eating nourishing food, but also in family connection and conversation.

The Family Dinner Project is a non-profit organisation operating from Harvard University, established to spread awareness of the importance of families sitting together to share meals and fun conversations. Their website says:

> Over the past 15 years, research has shown what parents have known for a long time: sharing a fun family meal is good for the spirit, brain, and health of all family members. Recent studies link regular family meals with higher academic achievements, resilience and self-esteem. Additionally, family meals are linked to lower rates of substance abuse and depression.

If one adult is often absent from evening meals during the week, consider creating special weekend mealtimes when the whole family can get together.

The following conversation games can add something fun and special to family dinner times. They are an easy way to encourage communication and connection. They evoke feelings of being valued, listened to, and accepted as a family member. This can feel important to children going through the 9-year crossing and entering into a period of self-discovery. Conversation games foster an ethos of dinner-time meeting, caring, sharing and enjoying each other's company. They are useful to establish fun conversations during mealtimes, and may not be required once communication flows more naturally.

The rose game

When a parent asks children, 'What did you do today?', the most common response is 'Nothing'! But if adults act as role models, sharing the events of their day first, children will naturally join in. To foster conversation skills during mealtimes, families can share their favourite part of the day. Or, to extend this further, play the rose game.

In the rose game, each person thinks of a rose as they reflect on their day. The parts of the rose remind them of things they can talk about: 'petals' represent an enjoyable or fun memory from the day, a favourite aspect or moment; the stem symbolises a new lesson, something that the person learnt that day; the thorns signify an event that caused sadness or anger – or perhaps even laughter. Take it in turns to describe the day, using each part of the rose.

Voice of a Parent: Jane

On Lou's recommendation our family has played the rose game for some time now. It really does work to create a fun and chatty meal time. We changed it to say that the stem represents something funny. We laugh together at the stories every day.

Would you rather...?

During the middle years of childhood, children are discovering their uniqueness as individuals. 'Would you rather...' is a family game that encourages personal discovery. Each family member takes a turn to answer a 'Would you rather...?' question, for example:

* Would you rather peas or beans?
* Would you rather cats or dogs?
* Would you rather reading or drawing?
* Would you rather travel by plane or boat?

Playing a few rounds during dinner can be lots of fun, and is a great way to connect by getting to know each other's interests and personal tastes, parents included.

Conversation starters

Some time ago, I encouraged a family to eat together around a dining table and to play the rose game. Recently, I revisited this family. The children are now 10 and 12 years old. I was so happy to see their excited faces before our shared meal. The two of them laid the table and encouraged everyone to sit down. They were keen to share a book on conversation starters for families that they used regularly.

The children eagerly awaited each question in the book, to share and to hear everyone else's answers. I marvelled at how this family's meal-time connection had strengthened.

Here are some examples of conversation starters, but it can be fun for children to think up their own too!

* If you could have any wild animal for a pet, which one would it be?
* If you could eat one food for the rest of your life, what food would you choose?
* What are three things that you absolutely love doing?
* What is your favourite book and why?

Tip - Riddles

I met a family who shared a riddle from a book each mealtime. It was a time to guess and chat together. A family joke book can be lots of fun too!

Gratitude

Another idea is for each family member to name one thing they are thankful for.

Grateful thoughts raise oxytocin levels by 25 per cent, and as oxytocin is our happiness hormone, this game has the potential to not only strengthen family bonds, but to make everyone feel good too.

Play the A to Z of gratitude, sharing grateful thoughts starting with each letter of the alphabet in turn. This is one of many games and conversation starters included on the website for the Family Dinner Project, which I recommend exploring.

Bedtime Rhythms

Until age 9, children are unaware that their parents cannot sing. After the inner transformations and growing awareness that arise at 9, lullabies suddenly become babyish, parent voices painful, and prolonged cuddles and touch may be declined. The bedtime rhythm in this middle-years period requires a different approach to that of early childhood.

Bedtime is an important transition time of the day. Children are entering into the unconscious, so it is a time for comfort, a time to feel safe and loved. Children's concerns often arise at bedtime, when they feel more vulnerable.

The following ideas suggest ways of connecting at bedtime.

Loving whispers

During the middle years of childhood, and if it's comfortable for both parent and child, whisper a loving message at bedtime. Once my children were in bed, I would simply whisper, 'I am so glad you are my son', or, 'I love you'. The middle years of childhood can include emotional ups and downs, so ending the day with a loving moment is special.

Voice of a Parent: Jo

My children were extremely grumpy after a particularly long day away from home. I took Lou's advice to 'breathe in'. We shared dinner by candlelight, and once in bed I stroked their heads and whispered loving thoughts with the candle still burning. I placed lavender drops on their pillows. The next morning my 9-year-old daughter said it was the best bedtime ever!

Gratitude diary

Purchase a diary or notepad and write a gratitude diary together at bedtime. When she was 9, my daughter wrote one grateful thought in her diary each night. If her mind was blank, I took a turn. This is a chance to share positive thoughts with each other, even if it's simply asking 'What did you enjoy about today?'.

Touch games

Some children enjoy touch games. Head rubs are often popular. I met a family who play 'kneading the pizza dough' at bedtime with a back massage. Pretend to chop tomatoes and mushrooms on a child's back and shoulders, then sprinkle on the cheese with a tickle! I have also seen children totally relax when a tactile object (e.g. a spiky ball) is rolled along their back.

The rule with touch is to see what children enjoy and request. Every child is different. Do not force touch games on children; respect their boundaries.

Voice of a Parent: Tracey

Our 9-year-old daughter asks to be lightly tickled once in bed. She says 'enough' and then falls asleep!

Chatting and reading

Conversation skills develop during middle childhood, and we parents are our children's role models. Simply say 'Let's chat!' for a ten-minute conversation at bedtime, and take it in turns to choose a topic to talk about.

If you don't have time to read aloud after school, bedtime is an excellent alternative. Listening to a parent read is a relaxing experience for middle-years children. Try to make sure the books are suitable for bedtime – avoid frightening or disturbing topics. Chapter 6, 'I'm Bored!', offers suggestions for middle-years chapter books.

Different styles

Jasmine, aged 9, still enjoys a piggyback ride to bed; Orlando, aged 9, likes a kiss and a cuddle; Charlie, aged 12, loves to join his mum in bed on a

> ## Voice of a Parent: Paul
>
> I have three children, aged 7, 10 and 12. My 12 year old is an avid and confident reader, and always has a book on the go. He reads entirely independently, but he recently asked me to read to him at bedtime. The other children have time with me before sleep and he would like some too.

> ## Tip - Timers
>
> Sand timers can be useful to indicate how long a bedtime chat or reading session will last, especially for children who keep calling parents back. Or they can be used with siblings to create equal turns.

weekend morning. Take the lead from children for hugs, kisses and tender loving moments at bedtime. During middle childhood, they are likely to swing between being loving and requiring more space.

Likewise, just as all children are different, so are all parents. Two parents will each approach bedtime in their own way: chat, read, touch – all these are an expression of love.

Every Family Is Unique

Daily connection times need to flow and not be forced for either parent or child. The idea is to bring enjoyment, not stress. Every family is unique, and ideas change as children enter each new stage. I think of daily and weekly rhythms as fluid rather than rigid. Daily rhythms are not immune to family struggles: morning grumpiness, meal-time fussy eating, and the occasional bedtime defiance. We are not aiming for perfection; there is often a bump in the road! Working these out is a vital part of family life and child development too, along with the happy, easy times.

Rhythms for morning greetings, resting, meals, chats and bedtimes may appear simple, but the emotional connection and stability they bring during the years of middle childhood should not be underestimated. These rhythms create profound long-term emotional associations, which can be of huge benefit in the future. They are one of the strongest ways we can assist our children during the Rubicon crossing and transitions of middle childhood, providing self-assurance, happiness and security. They help children learn to trust us, which is vital when we face challenging times. Daily rhythms also create a platform of communication and closeness before the teenage years. The suggestions in this chapter can be a guide, but you will have your own ideas and traditions too. Weekly and yearly rhythms also strengthen family bonds, and they are covered in the next chapter.

In Brief: Daily Connections

* Start the day with a few loving words – like the warmth of the sun.
* If you have time, set aside twenty minutes to eat, drink and share a good chapter book with children after school.
* Place a vase of flowers and a candle on the dining table. This is the place to build the family tribe.
* Play the rose game tonight. Parents go first so they can model family conversation.
* Family conversation games are fun. If children refuse to join in, try playing without them – they can join in another day.
* Would your child enjoy loving whispers, a quiet chat, or a gratitude diary at bedtime – or all three?
* Some children prefer less touching during the middle years, others still enjoy loving hugs and kisses. Follow your child's lead without judgement.
* Place phones in a basket up high so children know you're present during daily connection times (especially mealtimes and bed times).
* The middle years of childhood provide a lasting foundation for connection before the teenage years.
* Try one idea from this chapter at a time. Every child and family situation is unique. If a daily connection time is no longer enjoyable, change to a new one.

CHAPTER FIVE

Weekly and Yearly Rhythms for Happy Families

As daily family rhythms are so powerful, it is logical to extend them into weekly, monthly and yearly cycles. Human beings live in a cyclical universe: the seven-day weekly cycle, the twenty-eight-day moon or monthly cycle, and the annual solar cycle. We innately implement cycles in our lives.

Children are especially sensitive to cycles of living. Patterns of enjoyable and predictable family activities feed the etheric body or, in other words, children's health and vitality. To gain nourishment on an emotional level, family connection times can recur within weekly, monthly and yearly rhythms, which will in turn promote a whole spectrum of positive emotions: joy, interest, gratitude, surprise, cheerfulness, confidence, enthusiasm, satisfaction, contentment, amusement and love: in one word – happiness.

It is my view that happiness is the most sought-after emotion that human beings can feel. The award-winning documentary *Happy* contains a powerful message about what contributes to personal happiness. Surprisingly, genes or temperaments influence 50 per cent of happiness, 10 per cent is impacted by current circumstances, income and location, and 40 per cent is influenced by personal outlook, attitude, relationships and interests. The most helpful ways to increase your own happiness include: deepening connection to family and friends, focusing on feelings of gratitude, being in nature, and engaging in exercise, craft and hobbies.

Consciously creating fun family rhythms directly affects family happiness. Through personal experience I've witnessed how family rhythms can transform children's outlook and their happiness during the middle childhood years and long-term. The following chapter provides ideas and advice to assist with implementing weekly and yearly family rhythms, and as a consequence, creating real and sustainable happiness.

Weekly Family Rhythms

Despite good intentions, in our fast-paced world it is easy for the best-made family plans to slip by the wayside. To help get into a routine, place enjoyable and bonding family activities into a weekly rhythm. I like the saying: 'Families that play together stay together.'

Weekly activities bring a sense of connection to family life. A weekly rhythm is an invitation to spend time together. When this continues through the years, it provides the glue that bonds family members to each other.

Food

Eating is rhythmic by nature, and sharing a family meal is a daily opportunity to connect. In addition to the suggestions in the previous chapter for making the most of eating together, ordinary mealtimes can be made 'extraordinary' by using a fun weekly family recipe. If your family has a favourite food, pick one day of the week when you'll always have that meal. It could be home-made pizza, a pancake breakfast, taco night, Sunday afternoon tea or whatever works for your family.

A fun weekly food rhythm creates a comforting feeling of routine and connection and is an investment in your family's future. Once children leave home, if they live close by they might even return for Sunday morning pancakes, or meet up for brunch. Rhythms run deep!

Voice of a Parent: Annie

Every Saturday I make a big batch of pizza dough. My three children each get a ball of dough to roll out, before choosing their own toppings. My children say that our family pizza is better than any pizza restaurant! They look forward to Saturdays.

Easy Pizza Dough Recipe

Ingredients (family of 4):

* ❋ 4 cups (500 g) plain flour (can be spelt)
* ❋ 14 g dried yeast (2 packets)
* ❋ 2 tsp caster sugar
* ❋ 1 tsp salt
* ❋ 4 tblsp of olive oil
* ❋ 1½ cups (360 ml) of lukewarm water
* ❋ Toppings of your choice. These can include:

❋ pizza sauce	❋ peppers
❋ pesto	❋ slices of pineapple
❋ mozzarella cheese	❋ olives
❋ basil	❋ or whatever you prefer!

Method:

* ❋ Combine dry ingredients in a large mixing bowl and add oil and water.
* ❋ Mix to a soft dough.
* ❋ Knead on a floured board until soft and pliable.
* ❋ Return to an oiled mixing bowl and cover with a clean tea towel. Leave in a warm spot for 30 minutes. During this time, prepare the toppings.
* ❋ When the dough has risen, punch it once to get rid of air bubbles and remove from bowl.
* ❋ Knead gently for 1 minute.
* ❋ Roll into a big sausage shape and cut into individual pieces. Each family member can form their piece of dough into a ball and then flatten it into a circle shape.
* ❋ Add toppings and bake in oven at 180°C until golden brown.

Easy Pancake Recipe

Ingredients:

* 1 cup (125 g) of plain or strong flour (can be spelt)
* 1 cup (240 ml) of milk (any kind)
* 1 egg
* Pinch of cinnamon and salt
* Butter for frying
* Toppings of your choice, for example:

  * strawberries and blueberries
  * lemon
  * maple syrup
  * almond flakes
  * or anything you like!

Method:

* Mix the flour, milk, egg, cinnamon and salt together with a hand whisk, until combined.
* Prepare the toppings.
* Melt a little butter in a frying pan, then use a jug to pour the pancake mixture in.
* Flip with a spatula.
* Plate and top!

Voice of a Parent: Ariel

As a child we had porridge on Saturdays and pancakes on Sundays. After porridge we all went fishing and made a campfire by the river. My sister didn't like porridge; I have vivid memories of her sitting in the back of the car with it in a jar. Mum would bring it with us if it was uneaten!

Taking it in turns to cook

Once they are 9 years old, children can cook a simple meal independently if they've been taught. During the middle years, parents may assign each child a day of the week to cook dinner (or assist). This weekly role doesn't just have to involve cooking, it could also include searching for recipes and writing a shopping list of ingredients.

It's also fun to bake lunchbox snacks together on the weekend, to prepare for the week ahead. This is another useful and connecting weekly rhythm.

Voice of a 10 Year Old: Erin

I love Sundays; I'm allowed to cook all day. I make breakfast, lunch and tea. I look up recipes and follow them. I help Mum with each meal or cook by myself if I can.

Games Night

During the middle years, children are developing strategic thinking, memory capabilities, and are learning how to be good sports (with a little practice!). You could choose a weekly rhythm for family board and card games to encourage these skills. In our house we chose that Friday night would be family games night, and it was a fun way to connect and start the weekend together. Chapter 6, 'I'm Bored', for suggestions of board and card games for children aged 7 to 12 years old.

Voice of a Teen: Gem

I've been playing board games with my family since I was little. The whole family plays. My great-grandma still plays, and she's 96! It helps her to stay mentally active. My grandma and her sister hold an annual Scrabble tournament. The winner keeps the trophy for the year. My grandma is a little upset, as she hasn't won the cup for a while.

We play games each Sunday together, and on New Year's Eve or other special family days. My grandma has a large cupboard dedicated to board games, and she knows all the card games.

Shared Hobbies

The middle years of childhood are a time to create, build, do craft and play music together. At this age, children have longer concentration spans and increased finger dexterity. Observe children to see their interests, and invite them to join in with adult projects, when possible. A joint project between parent and child can easily be placed within a weekly rhythm. This project might involve craft, sewing, knitting, mosaic, cooking, gardening or woodworking, learning a piece of music together, practising a sport, or joining in with another parent interest, such as models, cars or stamp collecting.

Voice of a 10 Year Old: Phoebe

My favourite thing to do with my mum is knit. I'd like to do it more often, but she is always busy.

Voice of a Parent: Paul

I was practising my trumpet before a gig, when my 12-year-old son spontaneously joined me with his guitar for the first time. It made me think how nice a regular jamming session would be.

Exercise

During middle childhood, children enjoy moving and testing their bodies. Choose an activity such as bike riding or dog walking and place it into a weekly time slot to do together. Which sports are enjoyed by both parent and child? Perhaps a family game of basketball, table tennis, tennis or even roller skating can be placed in a weekly rhythm. This means that adults keep active too!

Parents may also take on roles in children's clubs – coaching, administration, and more.

Voice of a 7 Year Old: Ethan

I really like to walk the river path with my mum each week, while my older brother is at taekwondo. We walk to the bakery and get a muffin.

Family Movie Night

Place TV time into a weekly rhythm to avoid constant requests and whining. Choose a slot and simply state: 'TV time is Saturday.'

Where possible, watch movies together and chat about the film and characters. Find older versions of films if you can; the scenes are played at a slower speed, the noise level is lower and the special effects are less frightening. Children also like to watch videos of themselves as babies and young children, as well as documentaries or cooking shows.

Common Sense Media

Follow the movie ratings guide through middle childhood and the teenage years to protect children from scary and adult images. Once children are older and ask to see specific movies, the website www.commonsensemedia.org is a good resource to check out a film's content, themes and suitable age range.

Tip - Setting Limits

Create weekly rhythms for activities and food you have decided to limit. For example, you could decide that the day when children can have once-in-a-while food (chocolate perhaps) is Friday. Clear rhythms help reduce battles of wills!

Chores

Friday is called 'Tidy Friday' in my classroom. During the afternoon, each student empties, reorganises and cleans their desk, and tidies an allocated area. After Tidy Friday it is time for 'Free Choice Friday', and children can pick what they would like to do, from a selection of board games, building and craft materials, books to read and drawing fun.

At home, a regular chore day allows all family members to be part of a team. Children may feel useful when they are given a role, and parents feel supported. The topic of chores is covered in more depth in this book in Chapter 10, 'Answers to Common Parent Questions'.

Voice of a 12 Year Old: Mimi

We take it in turns to do the dishes. I am happy to do the dishes if I can listen to music while I wash up.

Bonding Time

Long work hours can encroach on quality family time. Create a weekly family date – like a fun appointment. I've met parents who give a two-hour slot each week to father-and-son time, or girls' night, to suit individual family dynamics. The predictability of this time fosters stability and happiness.

A weekly one-on-one date is particularly good for parents who work long hours or are often away from home. This regular getting together allows time to have fun and connect, even when life is busy.

To get to know each other in a fun way, perhaps pick a question out of a communication jar. Here are some examples:

* What is your favourite colour and why?
* What is your favourite food and why?
* If you could fly anywhere in the world right now, where would it be and why?

During bonding time, turn all phones and devices off and focus solely on listening and one-on-one connection. Create a vision board together of enjoyable activities: bike riding, fishing, playing card games, cooking a new meal, learning to play chess, completing a project, visiting a museum or eating out at a restaurant together. Then each week you can turn to your vision board and choose an activity to try.

Tip - Monthly Rhythms

Families can also create a vision board of monthly special activities to do together: tenpin bowling, visiting the zoo, ice-skating, a family picnic and game of cricket, or a beach trip. Write each idea out on a piece of paper, and place them in a family fun jar. Pick one out each month and have an outing.

Voice of a Parent: Kirrilee

I have five children, varying in age from 5 to 21 years old. I try and find time for a one-on-one date with each of my children every month. I find things in common that we both enjoy. These activities change for each child. They key is just being together. I let them choose the outing.

Yearly Rhythms

Some of the most memorable family times happen in yearly rhythms, including birthdays and festivals like Christmas, Easter, Hanukkah, Diwali and Ramadan, as well as holidays or seasonal outings. Family traditions for particular times of year form childhood memories and often get passed along from one generation to the next.

In my opinion, yearly festivals of all religions have their roots in LOVE. They provide a time to join as families, to share special meals, connect and bring magic to family life. Children become more involved in the festival preparation during middle childhood as they begin to take on greater responsibility.

Voice of a Parent: Melissa

At Easter time, my children help dye the eggs for the family egg-tapping game. Each person taps the egg of another to see whose egg cracks first. Children during the middle years enjoy this game as they have a better handle on winning and losing and competition than young ones.

Now they're older, my two children enjoy surprising the younger children by hiding eggs for the Easter egg hunt.

Birthdays

During the middle years of childhood, children still enjoy the Birthday Spiral celebration. On the eve of your child's birthday, once they are in bed, clear a small table in your home and cover it with a beautiful coloured cloth. Then add the birthday spiral (a circle or spiral of candles, perhaps tea lights in glass jars). Use the same number of candles as the child's birthday age. Surround the spiral of candles with photos of the birthday child with their loved ones at various ages, as well as decorative items such as crystals or a vase of flowers.

On the birthday, the family gathers together around the birthday child and as each candle is lit, someone shares a special memory or short story about the birthday child during each year of their life: 'When you were 1...', 'When you were 2...' and so on. The birthday child is honoured and celebrated as a unique soul on the earth.

Birthday treasure hunt

A birthday treasure hunt with clues can be a fun and connecting game during the middle years. Write clues the night before – a sibling can secretly help too. The first clue could read: 'I am hungry – woof!' and then hide the next clue under the dog bowl, and so on. Write five or so clues and place them around the house, with the final clue leading to the presents. Children can write birthday treasure hunt clues for their parents too!

The gift of giving

Children during the middle years are developing writing skills, which can be handily utilised for special tasks. A good Christmas or birthday present idea is for children to create vouchers for loved ones. This is the gift of giving from children's hands. Let children use their imagination, but examples could include:

* ❋ I offer the recipient of this voucher a car wash.
* ❋ This is a voucher for breakfast in bed.
* ❋ I will give you a ten-minute massage.

Christmas time

During childhood, even when children know the truth regarding Father Christmas, it is still a time of family connection, games and rhythms. Encouarge children to make their own cards, help to bake Christmas offerings, and decorate the tree together with loved ones. Include a new family board game as a gift under the tree each year, to fill the holiday period with fun and laughter. Consider including a craft kit and a new book to share together as stocking fillers too.

On New Year's Eve, create a 'games night' atmosphere and play charades and other fun games. Each festival is an opportunity for middle-years childen to join in with the preparations and to bring family connection games into a yearly rhythm.

Holidays

Many families already have a yearly holiday rhythm. Breaks from work and school form predictable yearly events to look forward to. They provide an opportunity to spend time away from the demands of everyday life and create special moments together.

I recently attended a funeral where the grandchildren spoke of their favourite memories. Each child reminisced about their family holidays. Perhaps surprisingly, it is the simple things that children remember. In this case, it was Nannie giving piggy-back rides in the sea, and picking apricots from the holiday house tree to make jam together.

Voice of a Parent: Melissa

On past family holidays, we have collected shells to make necklaces, been on long beach walks, and buried each other in the sand. Sandcastles became more elaborate over the years, with tunnels and turrets, and whole sand towns were created as the children grew! To be in nature, with no deadlines or time constraints, means living in the 'now', allowing a wonderful feeling of timelessness.

Tip - Magical Mystery Adventures

Surprise the family with a magical mystery adventure. Once a year pack up the car and, without telling them where they are going, take everyone to a special location for a fun family day out.

What Do Children Want?

I find it interesting to ask children, 'What would you like to do more of with your mum or dad?' The answers can always be placed into a weekly, monthly or yearly rhythm. Here are some examples of responses from children:

* Lucy (aged 12): I would like to go on more adventures as a family. To the beach, dinner, the city, the zoo. I like to try new things that are fun and interesting.
* Poppy (aged 10): I would like to spend more time cooking, crafting and playing board games with my mum.
* Charlie (aged 12): I would like to play tennis, go bike riding and play more board games. I enjoy learning new skills with my mum. I'd like my mum to include me in training the dog.
* Luca (aged 10): I would like to visit nature more with my mum, and look for tadpoles.
* Ethan and Jai (aged 7): I'd like to go to the park and kick the football with my dad.

Ask your children this question and see what their response is. Rhythms stem from the impulses of children. Parents need to attune to children's interests and pleasures. The above ideas are a guide, but new ideas are wonderful, and are uniquely personal to you and your family.

Let's Be Realistic

Family rhythms are not immune to arguments, tears, frustrations, and the occasional angry word by either parent or child. But the happy times often outweigh these moments. Let's choose fun daily, weekly and yearly activities that are manageable and enjoyable for all, and not stressful.

Rhythms do not mean rigidity. They change over time as children grow older and new interests or life circumstances arise. Sometimes plans have to change — that's life.

Spontaneity is important in family life too! Only a couple of rhythms are required, then you can go with the flow on other days.

Voice of a Parent: Julie

We live in rented accommodation and we housesit, so we move often. Daily and weekly rhythms are fundamental to our family life, as they provide the 'home' feeling wherever we live. We light a candle and say a blessing before each meal, regardless of the change in dinner table. Pancake Sunday is our favourite weekly rhythm: we prepare the pancakes as a team and eat breakfast together. Thursday night is 'girls' night' for me and my older daughter.

Our regular family activities are simple, but important. To create a sense of 'home' is more than bricks and a roof for us, it is our rhythmical way of family life.

The Glue that Binds

Daily, weekly, monthly and yearly rhythms provide the glue that binds family members together. Families that maintain some daily and weekly rhythms are more likely to stay connected. Rhythmical activities are anchored within children during the middle years, and so as children move into the teenage years, they may still participate in a few key family activities while seeking greater independence. Introducing and maintaining just one simple, fun and predictable family weekly rhythm makes all the difference for sustained connection in the long term.

In Brief: Weekly and Yearly Rhythms for Happy Families

* Which activities create family happiness for everyone – nature, exercise, games, crafts, music? Make sure they are included in your weekly rhythm.
* Why not try making pizza dough or pancakes this weekend?
* Games night means family fun!
* Weekly chores are more fun with music!
* Place limited activities into a weekly time slot.
* Create a vision board of activities to put into a monthly outing jar.
* Try out a magical mystery adventure together every year.
* Include fun yearly rhythms for birthdays and other festivals.
* Ask children 'What are the activities you would like us to do together?' Listen carefully to the answer.

CHAPTER SIX

"I'm Bored!" - Games, Reading, Craft, Building and Movement Ideas

After the Rubicon changes, parents may hear the phrase, 'I'm bored' more frequently, in addition to requests to plug into technology for entertainment. In answer, parents can encourage activities that foster creativity, strategic planning and thinking, fine- and gross-motor dexterity, and life skills. A keen interest in creative activities and hobbies during middle childhood is the ideal foundation to foster creative thinking in later life.

Creative childhood projects promote innovative thinking skills. I once read an interview with a successful entrepreneur who commented on his childhood knitting projects, the general theme being: 'If you can knit a pair of socks, later in life you feel you can create anything!'

The middle years of childhood are an important time for the formation of neural pathways. After 9 years it is almost as though the brain power that younger children devote to imagination is diverted to creative thinking. Creative thought processes become elaborate and multi-dimensional. Many children's activities assist this growth. Reading creates internal pictures and imaginative worlds; building projects inherently require science concepts during play; games create opportunities to communicate – to ask questions and work in teams; craft activities develop focus, patience, and problem-solving ideas; exercise and movement games develop gross-motor skills and the resilience required to persist with challenges.

In this chapter, I will suggest a range of activities that encourage creative thinking skills during the middle years, and provide parents with many possible responses to cries of 'I'm bored!'.

Board and Card Games

Board and card games are not only fun for parents and children, they can also teach important skills: how to think ahead, strategise, process emotional tension over winning and losing, work under pressure and be part of a team. Children are taught the rules and spirit of playing games through observing and learning from family members and peers – the key is to shift the emphasis from winning to having fun as a family. Card games are very popular with 9-year-old children, and a pack of cards offers hundreds of game possibilities. The most enjoyable and well known include Go Fish, Snap and Rummy, but the pocket book *Card Games to Play* by Phillip Clarke (Usborne) is highly recommended for more ideas. This small book can provide a lifetime of family card game fun!

The most popular board games for 7 year olds include: Trouble, Guess Who? and Connect Four. 9 year olds and older enjoy Uno, Pictionary, Game of Life, draughts or checkers, Monopoly, Junior Scrabble and Rat-a-Tat Cat, while 10 to 12 year olds often relish the challenge of chess.

Board games and cards can be a fun way to encourage children to help each other and to not take games too seriously. Keep in mind that a quiet word to reinforce the concept that 'Real winners have fun!' may be required from time to time.

It is possible to find board games based on co-operation rather than on competition. They are an excellent way to build teamwork skills. A Canadian company called Family Pastimes specialise in this kind of game. They have themes for all ages, including: house building, visiting the moon and tracking animals. The nature-based co-operative game Wildcraft: A Herbal Adventure Game from the American company Learning Herbs has been recommended to me by parents. It allows children to gain knowledge of edible plants and healing herbs while having fun.

Board games are often sold in charity shops, and they are a cheap activity when bought second-hand.

Many other kinds of games, such as hide and seek and charades, require no money or equipment at all. Changes is a less well-known game, but a lot of fun: one family member leaves the room and changes something about their appearance, for example they roll down a sock or take their watch off. When they re-enter the room, a guessing game begins: What has changed?

Voice of a 12 Year Old: Zac

I really enjoy playing chess with my dad; it is one of my favourite things to do.

Tip - Non-competitive Chess

When playing chess, try turning the board around every ten minutes! This puts the focus on learning and enjoying the game rather than winning.

Books

After the 9-year crossing, days can feel longer to middle-years children. If technology has not taken over their leisure time, reading often flourishes.

The use of imagination while reading is critical in developing children's interpretation skills and conceptualising and formulating ideas. Books contain central characters that are often archetypal, and these shorthand 'images' create an impression on a child's inner being. Depending on the quality of the story, morals are imprinted into the child's consciousness, which influences the development of their sense of right and wrong.

Moral issues are a key component of many books for 7 to 12 year olds, who are beginning to form a clearer and more realistic vision of the world around them. Books for this age group also deal with issues the readers themselves may be experiencing, and can be a useful way to help children process events, thoughts and emotions, as well as kickstarting conversations with parents. Aside from the developmental benefits of reading, sharing stories with children can foster a life-long love of reading and a genuine curiosity about the world. Put simply, good books nourish the soul.

Once children can read independently, it is still lovely to read to them after school or at bedtime. Take it in turns to read a page each, or highlight easy words for children to read. Take the time to explain any words they do not understand.

Voice of a Parent: Chloe

We are reading the *Famous Five* series at bedtime. If my partner puts the children to bed, I can't resist standing at the door to hear the story unfold. If my partner works late, he asks what happened next in the story once he's home.

The lists of recommended books for middle-years children below are just a guide, and by no means exhaustive. There are lots of wonderful books out there for parents and children to discover together. Thank you to all the children who shared their favourite books with me for this list, and to Melissa from Honeybee Toys and Books for her guidance.

Classic books are often best read aloud to children. You can find many cheaply in second-hand bookshops; look for books appropriate for children a bit older than your children's current age so you can buy ahead. Older children often like to revisit favourite books that were read to them at an earlier age and discover them again independently. My son read all twenty-one of Enid Blyton's *Famous Five* books three times over during middle childhood.

For ease of use, book suggestions have been split into age groups, but take a prior look at each one to ensure it is appropriate for your own children.

Some recommended books to read to 7 year olds

* *Olga da Polga* written by Michael Bond (also the author of *Paddington Bear*) is a fun series of stories about an adventurous guinea pig.
* Enid Blyton is a favourite children's author. The following books are well loved by 7 year olds: the *Faraway Tree* series; the *Wishing-Chair* collection; the *Mr Galliano's Circus* series; *Children of Willow Tree Farm* and *The Cherry Tree Farm*.
* *Milly-Molly-Mandy* by Joyce Lankester Brisley features simple and enchanting stories about a girl who lives with her mum and dad, grandma and granddad, aunty and uncle.
* *Teddy Robinson* by Joan G. Robinson is my favourite children's chapter book.

* *Now We Are Six* from the Winnie the Pooh series by A.A. Milne is a classic children's book.
* *The Seven-Year-Old Wonder Book* by Isabel Wyatt is full of magical tales.
* *An Illustrated Treasury of Grimm's Fairy Tales* published by Floris Books is great to read aloud and is beautifully illustrated. Fairy tales are a treasure chest of hidden archetypal wisdom.

Some recommended books for 8 year olds

* *Stig of the Dump* by Clive King is a wonderful portrayal of childhood friendship.
* *Charlotte's Web* by E.B. White is also a tale of friendship, this time of the farmyard animal variety. Also by E.B. White, *Stuart Little* is a wonderfully imaginative book about a small mouse on a very big adventure.
* Roald Dahl's books are classics, and enjoyed by children around the world. Favourites include: *Charlie and the Chocolate Factory, Charlie and the Great Glass Elevator, James and the Giant Peach, The BFG, Fantastic Mr Fox, George's Marvellous Medicine, The Witches* and *Matilda*.
* *The King of Ireland's Son* by Padraic Colum is an Irish folk tale with strong archetypes that is often told in Steiner-Waldorf schools. A book to read to children rather than for them to read to themselves.
* *The Celtic Dragon Myth* by John Francis Campbell is a Scottish folk tale involving dragons, mermaids and giants. This is best read aloud to children.
* *Aesop's Fables* is probably the world's best-known collection of morality fables. Aesop was a Greek slave and storyteller in the sixth century, and his stories originated as oral tales (as with the Brothers Grimm fairy tales).
* *Magical Wonder Tales: King Beetle-Tamer and Other Stories* by Isabel Wyatt is full of kings, unicorns, fairies and palaces, as well as heroic deeds.
* *Tales from African Dreamtime* by Magdalene Sacranie is a collection of magical folk tales from African traditions.
* *The Story of Jumping Mouse* by John Steptoe is based on a Native

American legend, and is the hope-filled tale of a compassionate and courageous mouse.

Some recommended books for 9 year olds

* Laura Ingalls Wilder's books are heartwarming autobiographical tales of pioneer life in America: *Little House in the Big Woods, Farmer Boy; Little House on the Prairie, On the Banks of Plum Creek* and *By the Shores of Silver Lake.*
* *The Wonderful Wizard of Oz* by L. Frank Baum is quite a different story from the movie. It is full of good deeds and kindness rewarded.
* *The Wind in the Willows* by Kenneth Grahame and *Return to the Willows* by Jacqueline Kelly are tales with wonderful language and archetypal animals.
* Enid Blyton wrote a multitude of classic mystery stories for children, including the *Famous Five* series of twenty-one books, the *Secret Seven* series, which has fifteen books, and the *Five Find-Outers* series, which also has fifteen books.
* the *Indian in the Cupboard* series by Lynne Reid Banks is full of fantasy and friendship.
* *Peter and Wendy* by J.M. Barrie is a book to read aloud to children. It has rich language, but as with most old classic books, discussion around racial and gender stereotypes are necessary at times..
* *The Tale of Despereaux* by Kate DiCamillo is a story about a heroic mouse. The novel is in four parts, and each section tells the story from a different character's perspective.
* *The Kingdom of Beautiful Colours* story collection by Isabel Wyatt includes tales full of great forests, golden lands and the star of the sea.

Some recommended books for 10 year olds

* the *Chronicles of Narnia* series by C.S. Lewis comprises *The Magician's Nephew, The Lion, the Witch and the Wardrobe, The Horse and His Boy, Prince Caspian, The Voyage of the Dawn*

Treader, *The Silver Chair* and *The Last Battle*. These books are all classic tales of good versus evil.

* *Alice's Adventures in Wonderland* by Lewis Carroll has difficult language, but is worth the effort as a read-aloud book.
* *Heidi* by Johanna Spyri is a beautifully written classic tale.
* *The Secret Garden* by Frances Hodgson Burnett is a moving tale of personal transformation through friendship while tending a neglected garden.
* *The Nimbin* by Jenny Wagner is a well-loved Australian children's book.
* the *Chains of Charms* series by Kate Forsyth includes six books, starting with *The Gypsy Crown*. The central characters are a family of travellers.

Some recommended books for 11 and 12 year olds

* *Black Beauty* by Anna Sewell is a very moving story, but also heart-breaking at times. Read ahead of your child and decide whether they are ready for it.
* *Treasure Island* by Robert Louis Stevenson is a timeless tale of pirate adventure.
* *The Neverending Story* by Michael Ende is rich with enchantment. A fantasy story for older children.
* *Legends of King Arthur* by Isabel Wyatt includes enthralling retellings of Arthurian legends.
* *A Series of Unfortunate Events* is a thirteen-book series by Lemony Snicket (the pen name of author Daniel Handler) that starts with *The Bad Beginning*. The series has a central theme that however bad things get, good things still happen.
* *The Butterfly Lion* by Michael Morpurgo. Morpurgo's books are great for middle-years children.
* the *Dark is Rising* sequence by Susan Cooper includes five fantasy novels for older children: *Over Sea, Under Stone, The Dark is Rising, Greenwitch, The Grey King* and *Silver on the Tree*. The books depict the struggle between good and evil and are based on Arthurian legends, Celtic mythology and Norse mythology.
* *Island of the Blue Dolphins* by Scott O'Dell is based on a true Native American story.

* *The Accidental Time Traveller, The Reluctant Time Traveller and The Unlikely Time Traveller* by Janis Mackay venture into the past and the imaginative future. The main character in the books, Saul, is about 12 years old.
* *A Roman Invasion: A British Boy* AD *84 (My Story)* by Jim Eldridge is a story for 12 year olds. There are a number of books in the series, recounting various historical events and periods from a child's point of view. *Princess of Egypt: An Egyptian Girl's Diary 1490* BC *(My Story)* by Vince Cross is also good for this age group.

Voice of a Parent: Paula

My son enjoys collecting books on interesting themes. The library is useful for this. He has studied animals and children's science experiments. At the moment he has asked to learn Portuguese, which is my native tongue.

Magical tales

Harry Potter is a hugely popular book series with both children and adults. My daughter's class teacher had a rule that children could read each book when they reached the same age as Harry Potter in that story. As the books increase in drama and scary themes in line with Harry's age, this was a good system.

The *Fabled Beast Chronicles* by Lari Don, published by Steiner-Waldorf press Floris Books, is an addictive blend of fable and fiction with creatures from myths and legends for children from 9 to 12 years. The first book in the series is *First Aid for Fairies*.

Audio books

Listening to audio books is a relaxing way to share stories from time to time, and a useful way to keep everyone entertained on car journeys.

I once ventured on a road trip of about 2000 km with my 75-year-old father and two children. During our journey we played classic children's audio books, and my father insisted we listened to them all right to the very end. He was hooked!

I'm told the *How to Train Your Dragon* book series is a fun and funny read for this age group, and an exceptional audiobook series for 9- to 12-year-old children. Recommended for parents and grandparents too, on long car journeys!

> ### Tip - Knock, Knock!
>
> Books don't always have to be fiction. During middle childhood, jokes are popular, as children are starting to understand different kinds of humour. Sharing a simple, age-appropriate joke book will give the family giggles.

Books before movies

Most classic books are made into movies. Make sure children hear or read the story version first so that they create their own unique imaginative pictures. To watch a movie version of a book does not require as much brain activity. When we read or to listen to a story, we create images from the words, which stimulates the brain's prefrontal cortex. We often hear the saying 'The movie was not as good as the book!' because our imaginations create our own character appearances and story settings.

Writing stories and letters

Children enjoy making up stories, as well as creating their own books. This is a wonderful activity for developing writing and spelling skills, as well as encouraging imagination.

Letter writing is becoming something of a lost art, but having a pen pal can be hugely gratifying for children, particularly if they are from a different country or culture. Even with the speed and ease of digital communication, receiving a written letter is a wonderful surprise.

Voice of a Parent: Carol

I recently started a daily journal with my son. I write a question during the day and my son likes to write the answer once he's home. It is a special connection activity that assists with his writing and spelling skills.

Craft and Creative Activities

There is no doubt that creativity is the most important human resource of all. Without creativity there would be no progress.

EDWARD DE BONO

Acts of creativity are powerful experiences for children. Craft is a form of magic: something new is created from working with our fingers. Craft also develops fine-motor skills, which in turn are critical for brain development. The inner being of a child is also developed through focus, patience, problem solving and individual expression.

The list below has suggestions for creative activities to try with middle-years children. Encourage your child to try a range of them, but if they find one they enjoy above others, give them the freedom to explore it: being creative should be fun, not feel like a duty. Crafts promote feelings of connection when enjoyed together as a family.

* Gardening: Could your children have their own patch of garden to grow vegetables or flowers? Or a long windowsill or balcony pot for herbs and flowers? Children also enjoy just assisting with garden tasks such as planting seeds or leaf gathering.

* Flower pressing: Create cards and bookmarks with pressed flowers and leaves found in the garden or on family nature walks. If you don't wish to buy a special press, just place the flower between two sheets of absorbent paper and flatten with a heavy book.

* Weaving: Make small weavings for cup coasters, bookmarks and doll house rugs with a weaving frame. Frames are widely available in good craft shops.

* Knitting and crochet: Create pom-poms, dolls and a multitude of decorative gifts. The techniques needed are quickly learnt with a bit of practice, and knitting has many physical and psychological benefits (see below in this chapter for more information).

* Woodwork: Give your children their own tool kit so they can help with tasks around the house and have their own building projects (e.g. a bird table).
* Whittling: Learn how to carve beautiful wooden items together.
* Cooking: Include children in daily and weekly cooking rhythms, and suggest they help compile a family cookbook.
* Origami: Find a good origami book in the library or use online resources (widely available with just a quick search). Making 'chatterboxes' is a favourite papercraft activity during middle childhood.
* Craft kits: There is a wide variety of ready-to-buy craft kits available for children, including making recycled paper, soap and bath bombs, jewellery, scrapbooking and paper flowers. Kits make excellent birthday and Christmas gifts during the middle years.
* Drawing: Children often find drawing a relaxing and sustaining activity, and there is no need to buy expensive equipment.
* Clay and modelling: Clay is widely available from art and craft shops. It is a satisfyingly tactile material for children's creative exploration.
* Photography: Older children love getting out in nature and taking photographs, which can then be used to make birthday cards for family and friends.
* Adult projects: If it's appropriate and if your child is interested, allow them to assist in your own craft projects, for example, complete a mosaic together, patchwork a family quilt or build something for the whole family to enjoy.

Voice of a 9 Year Old: Levi

I love playing with clay; it is my favourite thing to do. My family has a wheel, and I don't go on it enough.

Voice of a 12 Year Old: Zac

I like to take photos of flowers, bumblebees and things I find in nature.

The benefits of knitting

As mentioned above, there are many hidden benefits to knitting. It is truly a magical task.

Once the technique has been learnt, knitting can have the same benefits as meditation. The rhythmical, repetitive motion creates a feeling of relaxation; it can reduce heart rate and lower blood pressure after just a few minutes.

The art of knitting is not only improves mood, it also develops motor functions, and it stimulates almost the whole brain simultaneously: the frontal lobe, which guides processing, planning and attention; the parietal lobe, which handles sensory information and spatial navigation; the occipital lobe, which processes visual information; the temporal lobe involved in interpreting meaning; and finally, the cerebellum, which co-ordinates precision and the timing of movement. The Finnish Olympic ski team harness the soothing effects of knitting. All members can be seen knitting small squares to help them cope with the stresses of competition.

In Steiner-Waldorf education, all 7-year-old children learn to knit, often with the help of an imaginative rhyme, such as: 'In through the bunny hole, around the big tree. Out through the bunny hole, away runs he!' As a playgroup leader, I often invited the children aged 8 and 9 to teach parents how to knit. The parents would feel: 'If they can do it, so can I!'

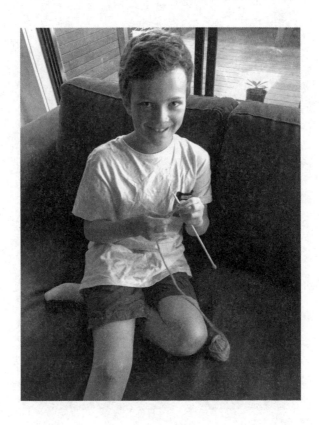

Collecting

During the middle years, children often feel a spontaneous desire to collect anything and everything. Collectable items include postage stamps, sports cards, stickers, coins and pebbles or similar objects found on nature walks. Children gain satisfaction looking over their collections and trading with others.

Voice of a Parent: Melissa

My daughter has a box under her bed full of weird and useful objects. She collects postcards, special bottle tops, wool and ribbons. My other daughter collects snow globes. I have a treasure box from my own childhood.

Nature Activities

There is something magical about the relationship between children and nature. Connecting with the natural world creates a feeling of being part of a big, beautiful and amazing universe. This ties to the learning of middle-years children: at this age they are gaining a stronger understanding of the world around them every day.

Observing bugs, leaves and rocks through a magnifying glass or microscope is a popular middle-years pastime, while looking to the sky with binoculars for birds and telescopes to search for stars is particularly suited to 10 to 12 year olds.

Voice of a Parent: Melissa

I remember how happy my daughter was when they were birdwatching at school. Every day she would come home explaining each new bird that she'd recognised. The children loved the binoculars too.

Pet magic!

Children experience pets as non-judgemental and loyal friends. With a pet, they never feel truly alone. Pets can be beneficial for mind and body. *The Times* magazine recently ran an article titled, 'Science Says Your Pet is Good for Your Health' by Mandy Oaklander, which stated: 'Animals of many types can help calm stress, fear and anxiety in young children, the elderly and everyone in between.' Indeed, most children's hospitals now have an animal programme.

Caring for a pet also teaches children rhythms and responsibilities. However, it is unrealistic to presume they can look after them independently. Adults will need to provide oversight, and carry some of the food and care responsibilities. Guinea pigs and rabbits are good pets for children during the middle years.

Voice of a 10 Year Old: Luca

I have a dog that just sleeps. I prefer my five chickens; they are very interesting to watch: one of them is the boss and top of the pecking order. I play with my pet rat every night. I am trying to teach him to fetch using rat food, but he eats the food without bringing it back! I have a fish, and it follows my finger around the edge of the tank.

Voice of a 9 Year Old: Jasmin

When I get home from school, I play hide and seek with my dog. I say 'Stay!' and hide somewhere in the house. When I call my dog's name, he runs to find me. My dog is my best friend. I also have five funny chickens; I like to write stories about them.

Planning and Building

Middle-years children love using their planning skills to build something, whether large or small. Lego is a popular creative building activity that also promotes strategic thinking, and is easily disassembled to create something entirely new. Similarly, Meccano is a reusable model construction system with slightly more advanced crane and pulley mechanisms to explore. Putting together remote-control cars and electric trains requires skill and control, as well as creative building techniques.

On a larger scale, building activities may include building a go-kart or a large den or cubby. To create a 'home' by hand provides children with a sense of confidence and safety, and is a way to imitate future adult life. Provide bamboo poles and large pieces of material to create shelters in the garden, or if the weather is bad, allow children to assemble a cosy den in the living room.

Voice of a 9 Year Old: Jasmin

I like to camp in my backyard and make cubbies in the local park.

Voice of a Parent: Kelly

My son put a tent up in his bedroom and slept in it for about two months.

Exercise and Movement

During middle childhood, children enjoy moving and testing their bodies. Co-ordination skills are distinctly more developed than in younger years, so families can enjoy movement activities together, for example bike rides, mini-golf, hiking, flying kites, playing with inflatable boats and roller-skating. Walking together is relaxing and healthy and a good chance to chat. If possible, walk to school, or perhaps walk the dog together after dinner.

Independent movement activities create healthy bodies, and a good foundation for life. Every child I spoke to when writing this book enjoyed bouncing on a trampoline. Movement helps to build children's etheric body, providing vitality, though it is worth noting that competitiveness can create stress, which reduces this beneficial effect. Children often start a sport after the 9-year crossing. Make sure exercise is fun!

Movement games involving skipping, hopscotch and hula hoops get body reflexes going and fire up the brain, and children can play them alone.

Four Square

Four Square is a popular playground game that can be enjoyed by two or four players, or by a big group of players. It's a small version of tennis, using only hands and a rubber ball or tennis ball, and can provide hours of fun and exercise on a miniature court.

If you have suitable flooring indoors you can mark out the four square grid (literally just a square – approximately – divided into four) using tape, or create a chalk court in the garden or on a driveway or pavement.

The rules are simple: each player stands in a square and takes turns serving the ball. It must bounce in another player's square before that player hits it back. When a player fails to hit the ball, or it bounces more than once before they hit it, the point goes to the opponent. You can also play in pairs or doubles.

With a large group of players there will be a waiting queue of players as well as the four on the court. If someone on court misses a return, they must wait this game out or go to the back of the line and the person at the front of the line steps into their square to have a turn on court.

Tip - Skip!

Purchase a long length of rope from a hardware store for some inexpensive skipping fun for your children. Tie the end to a door handle or chair to swing the rope solo. Buy small ropes for independent children skipping.

Games of skipping, hopscotch and hula hoops all integrate body reflexes and fire up the brain.

Voice of a 9 Year Old: Ilija

I love to go mountain biking with my dad. We go on much longer rides now.

Music

Playing a musical instrument uses both the left and the right sides of the brain. Fine-motor development, reading music, plus a will to practise naturally stimulate the left and logical side of the brain. Harmonies have a profound impact on human emotions, and being creative with music stimulates the right side of the brain.

The Steiner-Waldorf curriculum supports and fosters music development: all 7-year-old children learn to play the recorder, and this continues throughout primary school. At around their 9th year, children learn a string instrument – violin, viola or cello – while class singing is incorporated into everyday school life.

The benefits of group singing

Multiple studies have found benefits for singing in groups, including raising levels of the happiness hormone, oxytocin. Even if the singing is not in tune, there are still significant emotional, social and cognitive benefits. Could your family enjoy singalongs – in the car, on walks, around campfires, around the piano? Some families play a fun game, where for a certain period of time they sing their daily conversations, rather than simply speaking.

Voice of a 9 Year Old: Ilija

My uncle is teaching me how to play the guitar. It is my favourite thing to do now.

Creative Mind vs Technology

The middle years may be a time when children increasingly ask for access to digital technology, particularly computers and tablets, during their free time. It is worth being aware that many studies conclude online games create unwanted tension. They are highly visually and auditorily stimulating and have addictive elements. They often leave children irritated and uptight. Some games lead to mental exhaustion, and constant competitiveness can create general unease.

Technology is considered in Chapter 10, 'Answers to Common Parent Questions', but put simply, developing our human creativity is almost always more worthwhile than playing a screen game. The ability to creatively think may foster this next generation's ability to advance future living standards and develop a more sustainable way of life.

Creativity Is Positivity

Pastimes constantly change with children's developing interests, the influence of peers and their age. However, parents provide the environment for ideas and activities to flourish and for children to thrive. Wait and watch; it is important for children to have their own interests, and *sometimes* be at a loose end: this allows new inspiration to form.

When my children were young, if they consistently said 'I'm bored', I would respond, 'No such thing as boredom with a creative mind!'

The creative thinking muscle needs flexing in order to develop. The ideas I have outlined in this chapter stimulate the creative reward system in the brain, leading to a deep sense of satisfaction for children, and this positively affects their moods.

In Brief: 'I'm Bored!' - Games, Reading, Craft, Building and Movement Ideas

* Include board and card games in family fun. Learn how to play a new game together.
* Fill your home with wonderful stories. Use the recommended books as a guide, or encourage your children to write their own.

* Purchase craft kits for presents and involve children in adult craft hobbies. Perhaps learn how to knit together – it's good for your health!
* Head out into nature to discover the world around you. Stargazing can provide hours of wonder for children.
* Allow your child to build a cubby in the garden, or put up a tent indoors to make a cosy den.
* If you don't already have one, consider whether now might be the right time for a family pet.
* Letter writing improves literacy skills. Is there anyone who could be your child's pen pal?
* What is your family's fun way to exercise together? Why not try something new?
* Play traditional movement games like hopscotch, Four Square and hula hoops – they are an inexpensive and fun way to keep children active.
* Are your children ready to play a musical instrument?
* Watch your children closely for new interests and allow them to explore their creativity.

PART THREE
What to Say

Part Three is packed with suggestions for those moments when we parents may be lost for words. These include times when we are confronted by strong emotion in our growing children, such as anger or anxiety; times when we need to set limits for them to be safe or healthy or foster respect; and times when we can see children are growing and need explanations and guidance about their bodies but we don't know what to say.

CHAPTER SEVEN
Managing Children's Anger

The middle years consist of many outer and inner changes for children to process: there are the challenges of daily school life and navigating friendships, plus the feelings involved in a growing awareness of being an individual, with comparisons to others. Add to this a strong desire for fairness and a need to feel heard, both of which may be difficult to ensure when family life is busy. All these changes and feelings can lead to emotional outbursts for 7 to 12 year olds.

New angry episodes can be a shock to parents, and children too. It's not easy for parents to witness children's anger, but working through strong emotions during middle childhood provides the opportunity to develop emotional intelligence and resilience strategies. While parents need to be alert to other possible explanations, it can be helpful to understand that some outbursts of heightened feelings may be a sign that children are going through the normal middle-years transitions.

All the chapters within this book provide a foundation for balancing children's emotions. Creating family connection and ensuring reassuring daily rhythms in family life, for example, are part of helping children manage emotion (see Part Two of this book). Children who feel connected to their adult carers, and who have a reasonably predictable rhythm in their days and weeks, balancing quiet times and more active times, are less likely to experience dramatic emotional swings. Good moods are positively influenced by love, understanding and connection, time outdoors in nature, craft, exercise, and thoughts of gratitude, all of which are discussed in more detail in earlier chapters.

Understanding Emotions

All the emotional responses we have require respect. Our task is not to avoid difficult emotions or repress them, but to recognise them when they arise and find constructive ways to process them. It is OK for us to be angry, and it is OK for our children to be angry, but it is not OK for anyone to hit, to be rude, or to cause harm.

Causes of anger can include an unfulfilled expectation or desire, a feeling of threat or powerlessness, a sense of unfair treatment, or an unmet need. At times, anger can be a sign that a situation requires change. That doesn't mean we can express anger in ways that are distressing or harmful for others around us.

Feelings are an immense gift, providing a richness to existence. It is essential to the human experience that we have a powerful life of feeling. And so it is part of being human to learn how to understand our emotions and feelings and channel them in a positive way. Every emotion has a time and place. It is human to look for wholeness, and to foster happiness, love and peace where possible.

Anger and the brain

The primary emotions of anger and fear are chemical reactions that register in the brain stem or reptilian part of the back brain. Emotions like these are processed up to 20,000 times faster than thoughts, to enable a supremely quick response in case of attack. Anger and fear exist to prompt us to fight or flight when we need to react quickly.

Simply breathing and focusing on the breath can slow down the super-fast reaction of anger and dissipate the emotional wave. Pausing and walking away prevents an escalation of the fight response. When anger is present, we first need solutions like these to help regulate it in the moment.

After de-escalation of the emotion, we need to move our response to the frontal lobe of the brain, by encouraging communication and reasoning skills. This allows for integration of the circumstances and the emotion. This process is difficult for adults, let alone children!

The ideas for managing anger suggested in this chapter can assist adults too. They have certainly helped me. The aim is not to be perfect, but to gain clarity around emotions, and to continually strive to integrate our feelings. Integration means we eventually find peace and resolution, where that is possible. This process takes a lot of practice, with backward as well as forward steps.

Middle childhood is an ideal time to practise managing, defusing and processing emotions. From 7 to 12 years, children are centred in the feeling world and the frontal lobe of the brain is under development.

This chapter offers assistance for parents in three ways:

1. A discussion of the triggers that spark anger in children and suggestions for avoiding triggers to reduce angry episodes over time;
2. A collection of practical ideas to help with the safe expression of children's anger, and defusing the initial emotional wave;
3. A description of processes that can integrate feelings and teach emotional development for the future.

We'll cover each of these in turn.

Understanding Triggers

Preventing feelings boiling over into anger is always preferable to dealing with arguments and heated moments, but this is not always possible given that children have not yet developed the tools to do this effectively and independently. By exploring the root cause of strong emotions, we can assess what upsets the balance of our children's emotions and devise ways to avoid these stresses.

What are the main triggers for anger? After speaking with twenty children, the top two answers are:

1. Disappointment, especially when parents change their mind, and
2. Sibling tensions.

I discuss these and other common triggers for anger on the next few pages.

Trigger: Disappointment

Children feel frustrated when plans and promises change. This is important for parents to know: our words are powerful. A hurried and stressful life may create distracted parents who do not follow through with their agreements.

Parents may hear the words 'It's not fair!' on multiple occasions! Children aged 7 to 12 are able to plan ahead and envision the future to a much greater extent than younger children. Excitement builds, and if plans are later thwarted or expectations go unfulfilled when events are cancelled then anger will escalate.

* If your children make a request or ask a question and you are undecided, simply state, 'We'll see', until a definite decision can be made. Try not to say anything more positive to avoid later disappointment.
* Create rhythms for once-in-a-while foods and screen time so children know when the answer will be 'yes' and when it will be 'no'.
* Transform the word 'no' for children's requests so that they do not feel constantly thwarted – see the discussion of this creative discipline tool in Chapter 9, '"That's Unfair!" – Creative Discipline Ideas'.
* When you have to say a straight no or have to disappoint children, make sure you explain why in a way that will make sense to them, so the situation feels less unfair and less random.
* Ask children if they understand the reason behind your decision. This provides an opening for further discussion on a key value if required. 'Swimming is really fun, but we can't go if your sister isn't well. When family members aren't well we take good care of them so they get better.'

Voice of an 8 Year Old: Saffia

I feel angry when my mum says 'No' all the time.

> ### Tip - Pinky Promise
>
> Children during the middle years enjoy the ritual of making a 'pinky promise', hooking little fingers. This promise is set in stone, so use it wisely!

Trigger: Sibling struggles

Siblings live in very close proximity, so it is normal for tension to arise. Competitiveness, feeling left out, not being heard, sharing toys, and personal space issues may occur from time to time, creating angry outbursts.

Many suggestions on supporting healthy sibling relationships and managing sibling arguments are covered in the chapter answering common parent questions.

Other triggers

Disconnection. In households where there are many siblings, busy working parents, or where parents are distracted by technology or by their own problems, children may feel unheard or unnoticed. If children have needs that have not been met, their angry outbursts may increase. Children require undivided focus at key times of the day: greeting, story time, dinner time and bedtime.

Authoritarian-style parenting. Using 'time out' as a punishment, or using any punishment continually, creates fear and anger within children. If a parent sends an angry child to their room in a cross manner, they may sit alone and harbour defensive feelings. These angry feelings crystallise. Instead, suggest taking a 'cool off' break, advising children to take up a calming activity, rather than issuing a punishment.

Passive parenting. Providing few boundaries can lead children to expect a choice in every aspect of life. Children can then become very angry when things do not go their way. If you think your parenting style may be contributing to anger in your household, read Chapter 9 for advice on how to provide positive boundaries.

Pre-adolescent hormones and mood changes. Pre-teens can move from happy to snappy very quickly. Remain calm and try to remember that powerful hormones are at play. If we don't pick up the other end of the rope, the moods may be short-lived. Chapter 10 includes advice on dealing with disrespectful attitudes in 7 to 12 year olds.

Temperament. A child's natural disposition can play a significant part in how they deal with strong emotions and feelings. Choleric personalities can be quick-tempered and often need some extra help with self-control in this regard. Ideas from this chapter will be of assistance.

Hunger and tiredness. Overstrained physical needs can severely affect our mood, even as adults! 'Hangry' is a real thing, so establish daily food and rest rhythms. Ensure children eat breakfast and have good-quality nutrition throughout the day, avoiding foods high in sugars, additives and preservatives.

Feeling patronised. Older children feel angry when they are treated as if they are much younger. It is difficult to adjust at times (I know!), but parents need to become conscious of their tone and decisions, and try to be age-appropriate.

Deeper stresses. The root cause of anger can sometimes be sadness or anxiety. Is your child dealing with a stressful life event, or perhaps a school or friendship problem?

Tip - Keep a Diary

If your child displays persistent anger, keep a diary and note down when strong emotions occur: write the time of day, situation and what triggered the emotion. What was the root cause of the anger? Is it one of the areas above, or something different?

Voice of a 12 Year Old: Lucy

Sometimes I just feel really angry, and there is no reason why. I'm rude to my family and I don't mean it. I take myself away and then come out to say sorry.

Expressing and Defusing Anger Safely

Even when we understand and transform triggers, anger is unavoidable at times. During middle childhood, children are beginning to develop their emotional intelligence and need struggles and practice to grow. Mother Nature requires humans to be increasingly resilient as they get older.

Emotions can be compared to waves; they will literally roll through us. We cannot repress emotions, or stop them because they are not convenient: they are a chemical reaction inside our bodies. Similarly, it is not possible to repress a wave, but we can learn to surf at times, and not be thrown around in the sea!

Strong emotions register in the subcortical regions, or the reptilian part of the brain at the back. It is important to realise that emotions are literally 'in motion' and will pass through, unless continually provoked or stirred – then they may build in intensity.

The suggestions below may help the emotional wave to move through quickly and without harm.

What we are trying to do as parents is encourage a gap between emotion and action. Create a pause to break the fight or flight response, and to create a space between feeling anger and responding.

Listed below are some practical ways to defuse rising feelings.

Redirection

If tensions are building, redirect a child to help with a task or focus on a new activity. If the emotion increases, stay calm.

Adult calm

If we add fire to fire, we all go up in smoke! A fire will eventually burn out, unless fuelled. Try not to add to the fire of your children's anger. Instead aim for a low, calm and quiet voice during heated moments. Take your child to one side, keep words to a minimum to avoid further argument, and try whispering or lowering your voice to defuse the situation. A parent can potentially inflame a situation or help to heal and integrate feelings.

Voice of a Teacher: Paul

I have one girl in my class who is really fiery. If she's upset, I approach her from the side, definitely no eye contact, and ask in a low, calm manner, almost a whisper, 'Everything OK?' She understands that I'm offering her support, without a public display.

Key words

To acknowledge and focus on a non-threatening question or an instruction can move the anger impulse to the neocortex of the brain to aid integration. This part of the brain focuses on language development and conscious thought. 'It is OK to be angry but not OK to shout or hurt others. Would you like my help? I'm sure we can find a solution.' Simply redirect the emotion so it can be processed in a safe way, e.g. 'Breathe...'

Just breathe!

The idea that our breath and our emotions are connected is deeply embedded in yogic philosophies. Breathing techniques can be successfully used to steer a course through strong emotions.

Breathing deeply and slowly decreases anger (and anxiety). Practise together with children: breathe in for three seconds and then out for four. Accentuate the out-breath.

A good breathing exercise for children is to imagine smelling a flower and then blowing out a candle or blowing a dandelion.

Breathing exercises momentarily distract them while allowing time to de-escalate and defuse any feelings of anger or anxiety.

I recently spent time with two siblings, the older of whom felt teased. I sensed an imminent explosion. I went to him, placed my hands on his shoulders and said, 'Breathe, these feelings will pass, breathe.' His face changed colour, his breath slowed, and he became much calmer.

Voice of a Parent: Louise

I tell my daughter to breathe when she feels angry, to which she replies, 'I am breathing!'

I answer with a smile, 'Breathe deeper'.

The pause button

The 'pause button' is a good tool for introducing space, giving everyone the opportunity to take a breath and avoid boiling over. This is especially helpful with sibling arguments between older children. Pressing the pause button shouldn't be used to freeze the emotion and bottle it up, but to break the pattern of cross words and actions.

Parents can role model pressing their own pause button as a way of demonstrating the safe expression of emotions as an adult. In moments of anger or stress, say 'I feel angry right now, I will pause and breathe and then speak to you.'

Voice of a 12 Year Old: Charlie

When my sister annoys me, reminding me to press my pause button works.

1, 2, 3 ...

Counting games often decrease anger, avoiding escalation. At school, for children between 7 and 9 years, I say, 'Let's count the zoo: one elephant, two elephants, three elephants,' all the way to ten. I tell children to breathe as I count and accentuate the out-breath. As children ponder why they are counting animals, they automatically calm down, because the brain has changed state due to a change in focus. I choose a different animal each time. This exercise requires children to visualise the animals they are counting, which uses the frontal lobe of the brain and helps to process the emotion.

Counting down has the same effect as counting up! Ask a child 'On a scale of 1 to 100, how angry are you?' Breathe and count back from that number. You will often find that the child has calmed down well before you have counted back down to one.

Kinesiology

When you are angry, place the palm of your hand on your forehead for ten seconds and then remove. The angry thoughts may go with your hand! Shake your hand to send the thoughts on their way. In this exercise, the hand is placed over the frontal lobe of the brain, which brings the focus there rather than in the more reactive brain stem.

Touch techniques may be shunned by older children, but they do work. When we feel anger, the body is held tight. With the use of positive touch, the emotional energy can move.

As a family, perhaps designate an everyday object to use when anger arises (such as an 'angry jug'). Move the jug to one side and playfully shout into it, to release tension and to encourage children to let anger out. This acknowledges the anger before defusing it in a healthy way. It can also create a giggle!

To simply move can be the quickest way to process a strong emotion. Ask a child to walk with you, complete five star jumps together, or move outside for a breath of fresh air, to help defuse strong emotions.

Voices of 7-Year-Old Twins: Ethan and Jai

When we get angry our mum tells us to take ten deep breaths while we put one hand on the front of our head and the other on our heart.

Humour

If you can feel tension or frustration building, use humour to prevent anger from developing. As a family you can decide on a humorous saying together. In our house it was 'squashed banana!'. If tensions were rising, we would repeat this funny saying to each other as a reminder not to take life too seriously.

Key humorous words act as anchors to ground children back in the present moment. Humour automatically breaks tension and makes us step back and see the bigger picture, allowing us to laugh at ourselves without judgement.

In our house, my husband calmly says 'falsetto', which translates as: 'Your voice is getting too high and loud, settle down. I will listen when you are calm.'

Safe spots

Older children may ask to be left alone or storm off in moments of anger. With my daughter, we walked around the garden one day and went through all the spots where she could hide and no one would bother her. I stated that however angry she became, she was not to leave our home or garden, as we would worry too much. One day I could not find her, and she was sitting in a spot we had pointed out. She just needed a quiet moment to take a quick breather from life.

Voice of a 9 Year Old: Ilija

If I feel angry it helps to sit on my spotty chair in my room. I just need time to myself. Jumping on the trampoline when I feel angry makes my head feel funny!

Witness and wait

If children display strong emotions it can be helpful for parents to stay close and simply observe in a non-judgemental manner, rather than suggesting calming techniques. This creates a safe space for expression and release. Simply say, 'I'm here if you need me.'

Once the emotional wave passes, deeper feelings often come to the surface. Children may say 'I'm not good enough' or provide other insights into the root cause of their problem. These words may be a surprise to a parent. Tears are common, particularly if the deeper feeling is sadness.

Crying

When we cry, the body produces endorphins that reduce pain and help to improve our mood. This explains why people can feel better after a good cry. I always tell my children, 'Better out than in!'

Visual reminders

Visual reminders can help teach middle-years children how to acknowledge strong emotions and learn to manage them.

A traffic light system can be a highly effective way of working through children's feelings. The green light represents happy and settled feelings; the amber light represents starting to feel angry or anxious; the red-light signals anger. When feelings are in transition, in amber, they can go back to green or build to red. You can come up with a selection of activities or strategies that help take your children back from an amber to a green light: for example, going outside for some air, looking at nature, stroking or playing with a pet, drawing, reading, squeezing stress balls, listening to or playing music, exercising, or taking time to sit alone. Ask for children's input to see what they find most calming.

If the traffic light system isn't effective for your child, try to invent your own. One parent created a 'thermometer' game for her hot-tempered son. He loves numbers. As the heat rises, calming activities are written on the thermometer chart to help settle his feelings back down, before the two of them chat.

Another parent of a 7 year old drew happy, frustrated and angry faces on a wall chart. She placed the activity ideas in the middle with an arrow back to the happy face. This way she can redirect her child's feelings without words.

Older children may be given a simple description of the brain. Speak about this topic during dinner-time conversations or a family meeting (out of the heat of the moment). Explain that anger responds super-fast in the brain stem. We need to slow it down to help us to calm down. Suggest regulation ideas. Explain that moving thoughts to the front or thinking brain helps us to express our feelings, talk to others and find solutions, where possible.

However it is achieved, always acknowledge and praise children for recognising their emotional status and keeping their cool: 'Well done for bringing your thermometer level down; now we can see if we can find a solution.'

Building Emotional Intelligence and Resilience

As well as reducing the number of angry outbursts and having strategies for expressing anger safely in the moment, we can help our children with their longer-term emotional development. We can support children in their middle years as they learn to integrate feelings. We can steer them towards emotional understanding, and towards resolutions and solutions where those are possible.

Express and affirm feelings

Encourage children to express anger safely with words. Expressing and acknowledging feelings moves the impulse to the frontal lobe part of the brain for integration.

Acknowledge others' feelings: 'I know that you feel disappointed; I would too.' Or, 'I understand that you are frustrated…' Use acknowledgement first, as it can help de-escalate the situation. Be aware that labelling a child as angry may increase anger in the heat of the moment. Instead, simply ask, 'Can you tell me how you are feeling?'

However, it is often easier to address strong emotions after the anger has passed:

* ✳ 'You seemed angry earlier, what's going on? Do you want to talk about it?'
* ✳ 'Tell me what's happening.'
* ✳ 'What would you call your feelings right now?'

Find the root

There are usually deeper feelings behind strong emotions. Anger is often compared to the tip of an iceberg, or the smoke from the volcano. Look below the surface; what is underneath? Perhaps other feelings – fear, sadness, frustration, disappointment, competitiveness, jealousy, pressure, resentment or loss – are the root causes of anger. Or simply feeling overwhelmed. It is useful for parents to look beneath their emotions of anger too, for the deeper feeling. In many instances children simply do not know what they feel. Do not force children to speak; merely create space and ask open-ended questions in a non-judgemental manner.

Finding words to express and acknowledge deeper feelings allows children to build emotional intelligence over time. This will support them in the adolescent years, when they navigate new challenges.

Parents' Voices: Josie and Dave

Our 8½-year-old child has begun to experience explosive moods. After much gentle and supportive questioning, she said: 'I just don't want to grow up.' And she started to sob.

Voice of a Parent: Paul

My 12-year-old son was unusually sullen and withdrawn. It was obvious to me that he was stressed. I sat next to him at bedtime and asked one question after another, probing gently as to the reason behind his low mood. When I hit on the right answer he screamed, 'Get out!' The emotion finally came up.

I waited a while and returned to simply enquire, 'Doesn't it feel better to talk about it?'

He admitted that it did.

Resolution strategies

Once feelings are regulated and expressed, parents can guide children with ideas for long-term emotional balance.

Voice of an Art Therapist: Jacqui

I like this reminder when dealing with children's anger: Regulate, Relate, Reason. This is a good three-stage process. 'Regulate' is de-escalating anger, using breathing, grounding and visual techniques. 'Relate' lets children know that you understand and empathise with what they're feeling, and lets children express their emotion safely too. 'Reason' is the last step, and is about being able to see the full picture and make choices to move forward.

Time to reason

After the emotion has subsided, children are more open to reason. Make sure decisions appear fair to children, so that even if the decision has not gone the way that they would prefer, it is part of a caring ethos. For example, you could say that it is your job as a parent to look after their health, or their safety, or that you have to care for everyone. Sometimes the phrase 'This is how our family works ...' is required.

Also, it is OK for a parent to change their mind occasionally: 'I've had time to think about it and ...' This can lead to a win–win solution.

Tell stories

Tell stories of what made you angry as a child, and what helped. Look at the child's situation and include solutions for them that connect to how you dealt with feelings of anger. Storytelling like this helps children know that they are not alone in their feelings, and builds a sense of connection.

'Stop! I don't like it!'

Encourage children to say 'Stop! I don't like it, it hurts my feelings!' if they are upset by siblings or peers, rather than exploding with anger. They should repeat this statement three times, with a louder voice each time, and if ignored, find a parent or adult.

Water off a duck's back

Weigh up the situation, and if a child tends to over-react, teach them the saying 'Water off a duck's back', which means 'shake off the emotions and move on'. This is a resilience-building technique. You can also use the popular Taylor Swift song 'Shake It Off' for the same response! These sayings teach children not to take life too seriously. If you demonstrate and accentuate the action, the child may smile, and will be less self-conscious copying you.

If children cannot shake it off, they may need to have their feelings validated, to hear a story or to feel appeased if someone makes amends.

Make amends

If someone has been hurt during the angry outburst, including hurt by verbal put-downs, encourage making amends in some way, to help the sad person feel happy again. This provides a clean slate for the future; it allows forgiveness and renewed connection. Parents can make amends for their angry outbursts too.

Using Anger for Change

Even the most peaceful families get angry from time to time. In my view it is healthy that families get angry occasionally as it may signal that change is required within the family dynamic. It allows unresolved issues to come to a head. If angry episodes increase, look for triggers and think about the best way to deal with them for your family.

I have offered many strategies for managing anger, as all children and parents are different. Try a few suggestions at a time. Given the scope of this chapter, I have simplified what can also be a more complex topic. If the issues you face are beyond this book, seek help for yourself or your child with a referral from your general practitioner to a family counsellor, child psychologist or children's art therapist, especially if there has been family stress and trauma.

Remember that emotional intelligence is not a destination; there is no end or final test. There will always be situations that push our buttons. Emotional exploration is a lifelong journey of discovery.

In Brief: Managing Children's Anger

* Consider the list of triggers – can you reduce the circumstances that lead to anger in your children?
* Is anger masking a deeper feeling of disappointment or disconnection?
* Does a discipline style require change?
* Try some tools to assist children: breathing, counting, pressing the pause button.
* Once calm, encourage the expression of feelings. Ask questions.
* Integrate feelings with resolutions and solutions for the future.
* Tell stories of your childhood emotions and solutions to help.
* Encourage making amends to create a clean slate – parents too!
* Anger is sometimes the precursor required to change a family dynamic. It can be a wake-up call telling us that there is disharmony somewhere.
* Every person and every child are different. Try a few ideas at a time and see what works.

CHAPTER EIGHT
Suggestions for Anxiety

Each of us, in our middle years of childhood, faces the Rubicon river alone. A crossing is essential. But what happens when a child freezes, not moving forwards or backwards? This is a description of deep-seated anxiety. Anxious children feel stuck in dilemma: the way forward and back are both impossible. Another way of describing it is that anxious children feel out of their depth.

Movement is required; the only way to help is to coax the first steps.

What Is Anxiety?

We humans have been given the gift of fear to help us escape danger. Fear is a survival mechanism. The bodily response to fear is literally breath-taking. When we sense danger, our physical reactions – the fight or flight responses – are almost immediate: a release of adrenaline and a cascade of bodily changes, including: dilated pupils to see with greater clarity; an increased heartrate to quickly pump blood to muscles; fast breathing to bring air into the lungs; and inhibited digestion so that energy can be used for the musculoskeletal system. The body is designed to react to fear very quickly, and then return to equilibrium. Natural fear triggered by an outside threat is a valuable human emotion for survival.

But we are no longer faced with dangerous wild animals. In the modern world, with its subtle human stresses, fear is difficult to interpret and integrate. Anxiety is a reaction to fear, often to fear of a future event. A mere thought can create anxious feelings, without the fear stimuli (or a wild animal!) being actually present.

Anxiety is a feeling; it is a reaction to fear. However, anxious feelings may become stuck, and if those feelings are not integrated by the frontal lobe of the brain, they loop back to the primal fear response, creating waves of anxiety, over and over. While experiencing this loop of emotion, the back subcortical regions of the brain are unable to foster intellectual reasoning and integration, or the ability to make decisions. This is the frozen feeling of anxiety. There may be quick bursts of anxious feelings or a pervasive anxious feeling that stays with a child for extended periods.

Voice of a Parent: Chloe

If I spend time contemplating past actions or future concerns, my anxiety levels rise. When I am in the present moment, I am released from this anxiety.

Anxious temperaments

Some children are innately anxious in nature. Children with melancholic tendencies may find life more stressful and require greater emotional support. All the ideas in this chapter will be useful, particularly creating a list for self-regulation ideas to try over time.

Almost all children develop anxiety at certain times during childhood. As social beings, it is a natural human tendency.

Causes of Anxiety in Middle Childhood

Middle childhood may see a general increase in anxiety, especially during the 9-year Rubicon, for the following reasons:

* The birth of the 'I' creates a new feeling of aloneness, and that may come together with fear of the future.
* With this separate sense of self there is an increase in comparisons to others and feelings may arise of not being 'good enough'.
* A new awareness of duality (good and bad) in the world may create a fear of 'bad' events.

* Understanding linear time brings a new awareness of the human life span, which may lead to concern over death.

The emotional effect of these changes can be exacerbated by a number of common scenarios, detailed below. Parents should observe the specific triggers for their children's anxiety, provide comfort, and help to implement strategies that enable children to effectively acknowledge and work through anxious feelings whenever they arise.

Scenario: Fear of the dark

Darkness is symbolic of the abyss, the unknown. What is on the other side of the Rubicon? It is very common to be afraid of the dark during middle childhood. This fear is heightened by an active imagination, and by exposure to adult media. Scary or dark adult media content can increase anxiety because middle-years children often do not have the mental capacity to rationalise what they see and hear.

Voice of a 10 Year Old: Alison

I'm scared of the dark. If my parents' background TV noise is scary, it makes it much worse. Mum puts on a meditation or music tape, which helps.

Feeling safe at night

Listed below are a number of suggestions for helping middle-years children feel less anxious before bedtime. Every child is different, so you may need to try a few different strategies before finding the one that works for your child.

* Light the way with a night lamp or plug-socket nightlights. Children will turn off their bedroom nightlight when they're ready; for my son and daughter this was after the 12-year transformation.

* A sibling can bring comfort at night during middle childhood. I often hear of 9 year olds returning to share a bedroom.
* Children love to sleep with dogs and cats. The presence of a furry friend creates a feeling of companionship, and provides a comforting weight and warmth to the end of the bed.
* Provide a camp bed in the parents' room if children are scared or feel sick.
* Use creative visualisation at bedtime. There are wonderful books and audio resources that encourage peaceful sleep, or create your own. Soft classical music or natural sounds provide calm and reassurance.
* Warmth, touch and scent are all sensory elements that can help with sleep. Cocoon children with a new bed canopy so that they feel safe. Add a hot-water bottle or heat pack under the covers, place a drop of lavender oil on the pillow, or buy a weighted blanket. Touch with slow strokes around the eyebrows or massage the feet to relax the body and mind before sleep.

Voice of a 10 Year Old: Jasmin

I'm not allowed to sleep with my real dog, but I'd love to. If I'm awake and can't sleep I cuddle my toy dog, Snow Dog.

Voice of a Parent: Chloe

When my children seem anxious or hyper at bedtime, I make up a guided meditation or sing soothing songs.

I start with asking my children to take three deep breaths and relax parts of the body. I ask them to visualise drifting up to a beautiful blue sky. A rainbow appears, and I take them through each colour one at a time. How do they feel in each colour? This question allows for scanning personal emotions and thoughts. To end, they imagine lying across the whole rainbow and feeling peace and love. I find this guided meditation allows my children to integrate feelings and emotions from the day.

Scenario: Comparisons and lack of confidence

During the middle years, anxious feelings can arise from children's growing awareness of themselves as an individual, and how they compare with their peers and those around them. They may start to feel they are too different, or simply 'not good enough'. Parents and caregivers can help bolster children's self-confidence by providing encouragement and support using the following strategies.

Encouraging confidence and self-acceptance

* Establish repeated family sayings to draw upon if required. Themes may include: 'Everyone has a gift to share and something they find difficult'; 'If you can't make a mistake, you can't make anything' and 'I believe in you'. Say 'Whoops a daisy!' when things fail, and 'At least I tried!'
* If my children put themselves down, I lovingly say, 'Do not tell your brain that!' or 'Don't listen, brain!' or 'Cancel that thought!'
* Identify children's qualities and praise them frequently.
* Tell stories of your own childhood and how you came to realise that everyone is both the same and unique. Include themes that humans are designed to learn through making mistakes, and that trying our best is what counts.
* Guided visualisations may be useful. Include white light bubbles of protection, and imaginary magic wands and swords of bravery.
* Read inspirational and archetypal stories together, including courageous heroes and heroines. Children witness how the characters gather knowledge, skills, courage and a strong will while facing their fears. Before the 9-year crossing, Steiner-Waldorf teachers share stories of *The Celtic Dragon Myth* and *The King of Ireland's Son*, which tell of overcoming obstacles. All ancient societies have numerous stories of heroes and heroines that can help children move through this stage.

Voice of a Parent: Chloe

If my child puts herself down, I say, 'Don't say that about my beautiful daughter!'

Voice of Parent: Carolyn

My son is 9 and has recently started to feel less confident at school. He puts himself down, comparing himself to the rest of the class. Every day I sing songs on our drive to school. I make them up about how wonderful my son is and how today will be a good day.

Everybody is a genius. But if you judge a fish by its ability to climb a tree, it will live its whole life believing that it is stupid!

ALBERT EINSTEIN

Scenario: Fear of death

It may be a shock to parents if a child suddenly asks about death and dying. This represents a new stage of consciousness, and reassurance is required.

Discussing death

* If the topic comes up, find your own words to reassure children about the spiritual worlds: that we do not cease to exist after death, and other family members and animals are waiting for us.
* Talk about the idea that no one is separated if his or her hearts are joined, even after passing.

* Each time you see a dead bird or animal at the side of the road, say a reassuring rhyme: 'Blessed be, may your spirit run free!'
* Create loving ceremonies around the loss of pets and loved ones. The body dies, and the spirit is free. Use the term 'heaven' if you are comfortable with it.
* Tell the Steiner-Waldorf birthday story, but turned around so it tells of the person or animal being called back across the rainbow bridge to the land of angels.
* Every parent has different beliefs. Each child will experience death differently.
* The 9-year crossing is a sensitive time. Children may require protection from strong impressions. Simple nurturing stories and words about spirit can serve as a comforting guide over the years.

Voice of a Parent: Fiona

My son is 9 and his grandpapa just died. He came to me crying during the middle of the night. His question was: 'What happens when I die – will I be nothing?'

Voice of a Parent: Sebastian

My 9-year-old son cries occasionally because he misses his grandma, who recently passed. It is a long drive to visit her grave with flowers, so we have made a special place in the garden, to talk and share with Grandma. Somewhere to put flowers, little treasures and notes.

Scenario: Friendship worries

Friendship issues may become more common during the middle years, as stronger peer connections form and change.

Dealing with friendship issues

* A lack of friends is only an issue if it causes unhappiness. Some children are perfectly content to have one friend and prefer alone time. Respect this.
* When children are unhappy, listen to their fears and concerns. Acknowledge that you understand, and reassure them that things will change in time.
* Look to see if children are being too shy or over-controlling or bossy, which may create friendship issues. Help them balance these tendencies without labelling, which can lead to self-consciousness. Instil a new behaviour, albeit subtly: 'Great leaders ask for new ideas and make sure everyone has a turn to choose the game!'
* Open your home for play dates and social times.
* Look to children who share the same interests as your child and organise meet-ups with their parents.
* As well as school friends, encourage children to see their cousins socially, as well as neighbourhood friends or those from extra-curricular clubs.
* Share stories of how your childhood friendships changed, but everything was fine in time.
* Coach children on how to look for other friends, or give them ideas on how to enjoy being alone, until new friendships form.
* Role-play how to handle tricky social situations, how to express feelings and how to walk away.
* Talk through friendship skills, and how to be a good friend.
* Children start to learn that it is not OK to hurt others' feelings at this age. Make sure children who are feeling hurt know to say, 'Stop, I don't like it!' and to tell a teacher. It can be helpful for them to practise this with a parent in a safe environment, especially if they seem hesitant to stand up for themselves.
* If a child experiences social anxiety at school, it is important to make it known to teachers, who may be able to help.

Scenario: Feeling overloaded

Anxiety may also increase if children feel overloaded with expectations at school and home. Dealing with the many transitions common during the middle years can leave them feeling that life is out of control. Consider how to simplify children's lives or drop an outside actvitiy that is creating stress in the weekly rhythm.

A child may also feel overloaded by adult images of the world. If a traumatic experience occurs and a child witnesses the harshness of the world, it can be difficult for them to digest, and this may generate anxiety. Talk to children about good people and kind acts to counter this overload.

Some children experience extra-sensory issues. Their senses can feel overloaded by, for example, noise, crowds and overstimulation. Being in busy environments may bring on anxiety. If parents and children are aware of individual triggers, this can help to de-escalate anxious feelings.

Techniques for Reducing Anxiety

Fear and anxiety stimulate the parts of the sympathetic nervous system required for a 'flight and fight' response. The body requires a 'hyper' sensation to move quickly and react. Anxiety is a heightened nervousness that continues over a period of time. To create balance and harmony once again, activities that stimulate the parasympathetic nervous system (sometimes called the rest and digest system) are required, to bring about a 'hypo' response, slowing the heart rate and relaxing the body.

Anxiety is a strong feeling, and without the use of supportive coping strategies, anxious thoughts can spiral quickly. Dealing with anxiety successfully requires de-escalation techniques: specific activities that bring anxious children back into their bodies and the present moment.

The techniques detailed below assist the calming and grounding process, enabling children to move forward. They help with general anxiety, as well as senses that are overwhelmed.

Voice of an Art Therapist: Jacqui

Anxiety can be compared to a car with its back wheels spinning in the air: spinning fast but going nowhere. We need to lower the car to the ground and slow the wheels down to start to move.

Children (and adults) need to practise self-regulation tools when they are feeling OK. Then they will be second nature when an issue arises. They become valuable life skills.

Connection to others

Unlike anger, where children like to be alone at times, when dealing with anxiety children usually like someone with them. It is important to talk to loved ones and not suffer anxiety alone. The message is: 'I'm here with you'; 'I'm going to help'; 'You are not alone'.

Voice of a Parent: Cindy

If my children show signs of anxiety, the first thing I do is increase our connection time.

Breathe

One way to experience the present moment and to stimulate the calm parasympathetic nervous system is to focus on the breath. This is hard to do while feeling panicked, so practise breathing exercises with children during calmer moments. Look at the breathing techniques in Chapter 7, 'Managing Children's Anger'.

Voice of a Parent: Fiona

My 9-year-old son fainted during his first violin lesson. He was so busy concentrating that he forgot to breathe!

Acknowledge and express

Becoming aware of our moods and understanding that we can change our general outlook is a powerful realisation. We sometimes need to be reminded of this – adults included.

The ability to acknowledge and express our emotions plays a big part in conquering anxious thoughts. Tell children that there is nothing they cannot speak about, and that no emotions are wrong. To voice a concern, feeling or emotion diminishes its power. To bottle it up only increases it.

Give perspective

Ask anxious children: 'On a scale of 1 to 10, how scary is this? 10 is being chased by a crocodile.' This helps children acknowledge and externalise their fear, and creates perspective around generalised anxiety.

Voice of an Art Therapist: Jacqui

We need to create space between the anxiety and the person, then the person can look at it objectively. It is very subtle, but if a child is afraid of the dark, I say, 'Darkness is giving you a hard time at the moment!' The anxiety is externalised.

I say that the anxiety is a friend who needs reassuring, 'Thank you, but everything is OK.'

Redirect to a positive place

Remind children of happier thoughts, 'Name some things that are going well in your life' or play a confidence-building game: begin every sentence with 'I can …' Keep this game going to and from school, and around the dinner table.

Courage!

Tell children stories about how anxiety always comes before an act of bravery or courage. They are all friends. The following books all feature characters who experience anxiety, and find the courage and confidence to overcome it:

* *Hey Warrior* by Karen Young
* *Justin Case* by Rachel Vail
* *The Invisible String* by Patrice Karst

Sensory solutions

Anxiety indicates that a child has stalled in their ability to process what they are feeling and resolve it. The initial way to deal with anxiety is to bring back bodily self-awareness. Sensory solutions (examples below) create an expansion of consciousness to the whole body, activating the parasympathetic nervous system, relaxing the muscles and enabling the mind to reset.

Voice of an Art Therapist: Jacqui

I encourage an anxious child to experience three bodily senses: 'Tell me one thing you can hear'; 'What can you touch right now? Touch two things'; 'Name three things that you can see'. This game helps to refocus the child away from the anxiety loop and bring them back into their body senses and the present moment.

The power of touch

If a child feels anxious, holding and rubbing parts of the body is a useful tool. To stroke a child's back is a natural, soothing gesture; to squeeze an anxious child's hand passes on an adult's strength. Pressing down on shoulders or rubbing the head can be quietly comforting.

In severe cases of anxiety, if the child allows, rub extremities such as arms and legs; sometimes it feels ticklish, but laughter can bring children out of strong feelings. If children reject touch, suggest they squeeze their own two hands together, or lie under a weighted blanket.

Tip - Magic Handshake

Agreeing on a fun 'magic' handshake can help if children are anxious about a social event. 'When you want to leave, give me our magic handshake.' It is usually the thought of a new event and the transition time that is scary, so the magic handshake might never be used, though the idea of it helps as you are setting out.

Warmth

Panic can cause a cold feeling in the body. A child's face may whiten, and blood flow may not reach extremities. Warmth helps to decrease feelings of anxiety and to break the anxiety–fear loop, as well as providing comfort. To foster relaxation, try warm foot spas; supply a hot-water bottle or hot wheat pack; encourage a warm shower or bath, or simply run hands under warm water. This will bring awareness back to the body.

A cup of chamomile or peppermint tea (or other herbal teas) can also be soothing. It may be the chamomile herb that helps, but wrapping hands around a warm cup is always comforting. Sometimes a simple drink of water holds a transformative power too.

Tip - Anxiety Aches

If anxiety is long-term, stomach aches may be a part of a child's daily life, as the stomach is shutting down to assist the body to move through fear. If the stomach relaxes, the anxious feeling may diminish too. Warming and nourishing foods that aid digestion, such as vegetable soup, herbal teas and porridge, can help this process.

Movement

Exercise and especially walking has a therapeutic effect, balancing the brain and increasing endorphins. Walking somehow feels like moving forward and not remaining stuck in the anxious feeling. Suggest a walk with an anxious child.

Voice of a Parent: Chloe

My son has moments of anxiety and anger. Suggesting a walk has been a revolutionary tool for me. When he is feeling stretched, I simply ask, 'Would you like to walk with me?' This allows him to calm down without confrontation. After we've been walking in nature for a while, we can chat without eye contact.

While angry, he stamps his feet on the ground at each step of our walk together. The stomping releases the anger; it is a kinaesthetic experience.

Grounding

Sometimes children literally need to feel their feet on the ground to break the anxiety loop. Suggest taking shoes and socks off, to feel the earth beneath your toes.

Cocoons

When the world becomes too much, creating a cocoon allows time for children to integrate emotional issues. Throw a sheet over a table in a bedroom and pad it with blankets for a simple den.

Craft

Working with our fingers in a repetitive manner calms the nervous system. Craft activities such as finger knitting, traditional knitting and modelling with beeswax can be extremely effective at reducing anxiety. The Finnish Olympic ski team are often photographed knitting during their downtime at the games – they understand that knitting creates a relaxed environment.

Other sensory ideas

Other sensory ideas for relieving anxious feelings include rubbing a few drops of lavender oil on the temples or wrists, popping some Bach Flower Rescue Remedy drops under the tongue, or redirecting children to an activity that brings joy, centring and balance.

All children are different. Look for the triggers to fear and anxiety, and try to identify which parasympathetic calming techniques work with your particular children. The long-term goal is self-awareness and regulation strategies that children can call upon during their teenage years and adult life.

Voice of a Parent: Kirrilee

My older daughter has a list to refer to if she feels anxious before bed and I am busy with her younger brother. The list includes: take a warm shower, make a cup of chamomile tea, draw, cuddle a pet and talk to someone. This practice is teaching her self-care and life skills.

Voice of an Art Therapist: Jacqui

Visit a paint shop and gather colour sample cards. Ask children which colours reflect different emotions. Choose colours that children relate to happiness and peace.

Once home, ask children to write down or draw any activities they know that help to create a particular positive feeling on the back of the card that they connected with that feeling (for example, if the children connected either purple, blue or green with calm, they would write activities they find calming on the appropriate card). Children can be directed to choose a card that will help settle rising anxious feelings and increase positive moods.

Resilience

Anxiety is part of child development. When the body learns to process and integrate fear, it creates new neural pathways in the brain. This assists in managing life's challenges long-term. To support children into adulthood, we need to encourage them to find their own solutions, albeit with initial assistance, and to move forward, holding our hands at first.

Naturally, parents want to help their children in difficult moments, but it is important to build resilience by not jumping in to save children during every minor issue. Let them know you will always be there and offer comforting and supportive words: 'You've got this!' or 'I believe in you and will be by your side.' Ask open-ended questions. You can always step in if you decide they really do need your help.

Voice of a Parent: Melissa

My child's teacher encouraged us to step back from small friendship struggles; to stay objective about the drama. I would listen and coach my daughter to come up with her own solutions, asking 'What do you think could help this situation?' or 'What have you already tried?'

Voice of a Parent: Julie

I became aware of my pattern of fixing my daughter's issues when she was either angry or anxious. Over time I realised this often escalated the situation. These three questions have assisted to gently guide a solution: 'How do you feel?'; 'How do you want to feel?'; 'What do you want to do now?'

When to seek help

If there is a sudden increase in anxiety, not connected to Rubicon changes or generalised anxiety, children require immediate assistance. For example, if a child is displaying signs of stress, sucking of hair, crying periods and out-of-character behaviour, adults need to step in to help resolve, support and make changes if necessary.

Children need to feel supported and heard. Provide an environment where children can express their feelings openly; ensure there is no judgement of anxious feelings: 'It's OK to feel anxious from time to time, it's normal'. Ask questions to understand the nature of the anxiety. Provide reassurance, and a possible workshopping of ideas. Communicate helpful strategies. Monitor the situation and keep communication open overtime. If the anxiety is related to a school issue, notify teachers. If you have concerns about your child, seek professional advice, perhaps starting with your local general practitioner.

The best support parents can give children is a safe environment for emotions to be expressed. Let children know that there is nothing they cannot tell you. Working through emotions can bring families closer together, and developing emotional intelligence and resilience is the best foundation for good mental health for life.

In Brief: Suggestions for Anxiety

* Anxiety is unprocessed fear, often of a future event.
* When children experience anxiety, try and stay calm as a parent.
* Middle childhood may naturally see an increase in anxious moments.
* It is normal for 7- to 12-year-old children to be afraid of the dark and require a light, warmth, cocoon, or another animal or person in order to sleep well.
* If children compare themselves with others, regularly use family sayings to celebrate that everyone is unique.
* Be prepared for a child to enquire about death – paint a simple picture of the comforts of the spiritual worlds.
* Help children feel secure with changing friendships.
* Ideas to de-escalate anxieties include: connection, breathing, touch, warmth, movement, grounding techniques, sensory games, cocoons and craft.
* Encourage acknowledgement and expression of thoughts and fears. Help to give your children perspective on their anxiety.
* It can help children to be aware of anxiety triggers and to know some calm-down techniques, as they may learn to regulate anxiety themselves to some degree over time.
* The first step to managing emotions is observing our children's emotional reactions and our own.
* Be there for children emotionally. Acknowledge their feelings and let them know there is nothing they can't tell you.

CHAPTER NINE
'That's Unfair!'
– Creative Discipline Ideas

'Discipline' is a positive word; I like to share its core message everywhere. It does not mean 'to punish', which is to create fear, blame or shame. This common interpretation of discipline is based on a misunderstanding that needs to be reconsidered. 'Discipline' actually means 'to teach' or 'to provide training'. Discipline is about supporting others in learning to live a happy, healthy and meaningful life. Discipline for children is about communicating positive values for living.

This chapter outlines ten creative discipline tools that parents can try when they need to teach or reinforce their family values. I have developed these tools in greater detail in *Creative Discipline, Connected Family* (Floris Books, 2015) my book on creative discipline and offer a summary version here, with special reference to the middle years of childhood. But before leaping to practical techniques I have some initial thoughts to share about discovering your personal family values, and about what factors contribute to a positive style of parental discipline.

Values

All of us need discipline, in the true sense of the word, to move towards our potential. There are many core values to aspire to. Let us consider a few that are immensely positive in family life:

* kindness
* love
* honesty
* health
* respect
* happiness
* balance

* security
* safety
* fun
* creativity
* perseverance
* gratitude
* compassion.

Add to this list yourself …

As an example, love, happiness, balance and gratitude are central to our daily rythmns of family connection. Other key values form the basis of teaching children how to live healthy and respectful lives, and to thrive in the world.

I can specify three values that are the mainspring for my work with children and creative discipline:

* safety
* health
* respect

I believe that almost all positive discipline flows from these three key values.

Safety, for me, includes being personally safe as well as being safe around others: doing no harm to any person, animal or object. It also means establishing a strong sense of loving bonds, feeling secure and safe, and being fully accepted as an individual.

We need to protect health when we make choices about food, exercise and screen time. A consistent and reasonable bedtime nourishes the body with good-quality sleep.

Respect includes an overall respect for life, for all creatures great and small. This includes a respect for belongings and for other people's feelings, as well as self-respect. It includes using respectful communication, and respecting people's differences. For children, it can be simply described as kindness.

All children, of all ages, require loving guidance and discipline in maintaining such values, and they require meaningful boundaries or limits in these areas.

Being clear about our own values as parents is essential to being clear and consistent with our need to discipline, or to step in and teach our children.

Discipline expresses care

When we discipline children, when we say their behaviour needs our guidance, it shows we care about a value that has been broken. And it shows we care about the children themselves, and about the other people around them.

My daughter once insinuated that I cared more about her brother than about her. She then explained she'd come to this conclusion because I nagged him more about eating vegetables! Nagging is, as its spelling suggests, Not A Good idea, but deep down my daughter understood my insistence on healthy eating as a sign that I cared about her brother's well-being. Children often see discipline that arises from our values as an act of love.

An Exercise: What are your core values?

Take some time to think about your core values.

* What are your wishes for your child?
* What are the values that make your household feel harmonious?
* What are the values that will help navigate challenges?

An exercise that can help clarify and affirm your values is to think about value words and then arrange them to create a 'vision board'. You can use an inspiring picture theme to structure the words. A tree is a good analogy. The key values can be written in the roots: words such as 'safety', 'fun', 'health' and 'kindness', perhaps. The branches can include descriptions of the ways we display these values in family life.

You can do this exercise yourself, or together with your partner. Or during a family meeting create a vision board with children, or simply write out key value words together. You can add a few family photos for inspiration. Ask children for ideas to create a happy home – this way they take ownership of the family values too.

The process of creating a vision board or simply writing down key value words can assist us in thinking deeply about our values.

It can remind us what we are striving for when we are in the throes of busy and demanding family life. Referring to a vision board or list of our values can be an inspiring way of returning to what matters most when family life is particularly challenging.

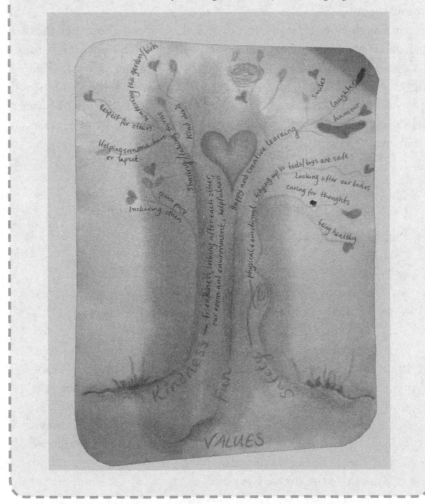

Communicating values

The question 'How can I discipline my children?' can be answered more effectively if changed to 'How can I communicate with my children?'.

We are less likely to have to deal with behaviour that crosses boundaries if everyone in the family understands the family values. And remember, one of the most influential long-term communications of our values is how we ourselves live.

When you see a value being broken, ask yourself whether that value has been communicated in a positive and empowering way. How can we talk about meaningful living without preaching? How can we encourage children to truly understand that their actions and words affect others as well as themselves? How can we develop empathy in our children and assist them in making real change?

Positive discipline for middle-years children

Children younger than 7 do a great deal of their learning through imitation and from direct adult instructions. Over 7, this mode declines. Rather than intuitive copying, children in the middle years develop their own deeper feelings and inner voice. This means they need to relearn family values not as an imitative process but as more deeply felt feelings of fairness and truth. They need to personally grasp rules and values, to take them on as their own.

An advantage of this stage is children's greater capacity to understand and verbalise their own feelings and thoughts. We can use these new skills in discussions of the family's values, and also to develop greater empathy – which helps enormously with children developing meaningful self-regulation.

Between the ages of 7 and 12, children are more often out of parents' immediate protection; they evolve stronger relationships with their peer group; they attend school and community groups; they are developing their own sense of self; they have a growing independence. Our aim as parents is for our children to live according to family values even when we aren't present to watch them.

So the middle years of childhood are an important time to embed core values. The prefrontal cortex of the brain is developing, which means children gain more self-awareness, an increase in language and reasoning skills, and develop a greater understanding of the cause and effect of actions overtime.

After establishing key family values for healthy and happy living, the best way to reinforce those values is through consistent, practical and loving discipline. Before describing that in practice, it is worth saying that the middle years of childhood involve a lot of learning, exploration and experimentation, which means outcomes will not always go to plan. Children will get themselves into difficulties and will sometimes make poor choices. A family philosophy can include that it is OK to make mistakes: that is how we learn key valuable life lessons. We can always make amends and create a clean slate for the next day. Forgiveness is a key value, too, towards our children and ourselves.

And parents feeling their way with positive discipline strategies often need to do some learning and experimentation themselves! Values are inspiring concepts, but living according to values is not always easy. It takes time and practice.

I have left this chapter until the final part of the book because in order to think about positive discipline for middle-years children, we must first grasp the needs of children at this age, their stage of development, and also how to stay connected as a family, which are covered in earlier chapters.

Discipline Styles

Having identified core values, we can think broadly about how to communicate values to children. Psychologists identify three main styles that parents adopt when it comes to discipline:

1. authoritarian
2. permissive
3. authoritative

Parents usually display one parenting style overall but also use a mix of all these styles at one time or another, perhaps tending in one direction when we are tired or stressed and another when we are relaxed. Parenting research suggests that the last in this list, the authoritative style, is generally the most beneficial for family life and children's long-term well-being. I call my version of this style 'creative discipline'.

It is worth thinking about parenting styles. If we don't make a conscious decision about how we want to parent, we often copy the parenting style we grew up with, or shift to the style that is the exact opposite of our own parents. It can be helpful to understand different parenting styles, and to take time to consider our own.

Authoritarian parenting

If a discipline style includes shouting, and focuses on rewards and punishments, it is called authoritarian parenting. The risks of authoritarian parenting are that children may not connect as closely with their parents; they may become defensive and withdrawn, especially where discipline is concerned; and they may learn to lie to avoid punishments.

Raising your voice occasionally, especially to highlight a strong value – for example, if a situation is dangerous or unsafe – is a necessary part of discipline and does not in itself constitute authoritarian parenting.

Authoritarian parents assert their rules and values with little discussion and often repeat 'Do as I say!', which can be ineffective during middle childhood, when children have increasingly more independent thoughts and feelings, and are more likely to demand explanations and fairness. When threats, punishments and time-outs are used regularly, children build an internal defensive wall as an emotional survival mechanism. And once children do not care about a threat or punishment, the authoritarian parent or teacher has lost control. Children are being disciplined because they are not respecting a particular value, yet the meaning of the value will get lost within a power struggle of cross words and defensiveness. This is not effective communication of values, nor does it help middle-years children take on family values as their own.

If you recognise that you are shouting a lot, take time to think about your own emotions. Are you stuck in a particular pattern? The creative discipline tools in this chapter may help you find other approaches to try.

Voice of a 10 Year Old: Sam

When I do something wrong and I'm told to go to my room, it's OK, as I like it in my room.

Voice of a 9 Year Old: Phoebe

When my parents shout, I just want to shout back. When they get angry, I just want to get angry back.

Voice of a Parent: Jonathon

I realised that I was shouting all the time. If my children's behaviour became disruptive or annoying, I raised my voice. After listening to Lou, I have more practical ideas to deal with challenges.

Reflection - Don't Sweat the Small Stuff

Choose your battles, so it is not always a battleground at home!

Permissive parenting

If parents are loving, but provide few or no clear boundaries to inappropriate or challenging behaviour, this is known as permissive or passive parenting. The risks of this parenting style are that children do not have healthy limits for dangerous or disrespectful behaviour; they may miss important lessons about safety and respect; and their behaviour may become anti-social at home, at school or with others, which will not help them as they enter the world. Avoiding necessary boundaries is not an act of kindness to children.

A permissive parenting style tends to treat children as little adults, giving them choice over every aspect of life. Parents are often left feeling powerless and exhausted, as every aspect of daily life can tip towards negotiation, and there can be a sense of chaos from lack of structure, limits and rhythms.

When children are overwhelmed, stressed or tired, we all veer towards a more permissive style of parenting – we are not as firm about breaches of values. This shows compassion in a particular situation and doesn't mean we are permissive parents in general.

Voice of a Parent: Jo

What I have seen over time is that children take powers and freedoms if they are given them, but deep inside they crave boundaries and can become quite unhappy if parenting is very permissive. People tend to think permissive parenting is what children want, when in fact limits and discipline help middle-years children feel secure and loved.

Authoritative parenting - creative discipline

Psychologists recommend that we aim most of the time for a middle path between authoritarian and permissive parenting styles. This middle way requires that we communicate and provide boundaries in a manner that is fair, firm and loving. My term for this style is 'creative discipline'. Rudolf Steiner spoke of the adult being a 'loving authority', and said such parenting gives children a renewed sense of confidence in the world and their place in it. Children require strong connections and boundaries to feel safe, secure and loved, and to thrive in the world.

How do parents behave when they practise creative discipline? What does 'loving authority' look like? In other words, how best do we foster values in family life?

Parents using this middle path of discipline:

* respond consistently to behaviours that are unsafe, unhealthy or disrespectful. The key value of respect for self and others is reinforced.
* view children's behaviour objectively, with an understanding of child development. They ask whether behaviour is influenced by the child's age and stage.
* contemplate the reason or underlying motive behind challenging behaviour. Why is this child responding in a difficult manner? What else is happening for the child?
* focus on solutions, rather than on blame and finding fault.
* help children develop self-discipline through self-regulation. They explain why certain behaviours are leading to difficulties in ways that children can understand.

* praise children's behaviour when they take responsibility themselves and display key values.
* expect positive behaviour, rather than deciding that difficult behaviour is normal.
* provide firm boundaries when key values are repeatedly broken, teaching children the cause and effect of their behaviour.
* recognise that creative discipline is training for life: not a destination but a journey.

Uninvolved parenting

It is worth being aware that in recent years psychologists have identified a fourth parenting style: the 'uninvolved parent'. When our lives become too busy, stressed or distracted, family values and connection are lost. We become disengaged from our children and from our role as parents. Being conscious of this twenty-first-century trap is not about feeling guilty when we realise we've slipped into it, but feeling empowered to make small but significant changes. Parenting requires time and presence. Children require our full attention at key times of each day, and for adults to step in when family values require addressing and reinforcing.

I recommend having a technology basket where adult phones, tablets and other devices are stored at particular times of day to highlight the importance of family connection time, and to stay focused on the path of parenting.

Exercise: Leaving stress behind

When you are returning home from work, five minutes before the end of your journey pull over or take time out on your commute to make a final check of your phone, emails and social media. Then, before you reach your door, touch a specific tree, plant or wall and leave all your adult stress there. You can use the same object each day.

The idea of this exercise is to arrive at home ready to be fully present in family life, to make emotional space for your loved ones at the end of the day.

A new way of discipline for the middle years

The three transformative changes during middle childhood, at 7, 9 and 12 years, are almost quantum leaps in childhood consciousness. Children are increasingly aware of themselves and other people, they are developing a new, wider understanding of fairness, and they are able to make comparisons between their own lives and those of others. These changes underline the need for parents to explain discipline decisions and the values underpinning them.

At times, parents can simply say: 'This is how we do it in our home.'

Children aged between 7 and 12 question the nature of truth. What is 'truth' and 'not truth'? They judge adult decisions and opinions. Family values will be assessed and, at times, tested. Children will voice their concerns and raise questions. This is not always easy for parents, but questioning is a vital skill for life and for intellectual growth that children learn in the middle years.

The following ideas help to develop meaningful boundaries amid all this questioning, so children develop self-regulation skills over time.

Ten Creative Discipline Tools

In the rest of this chapter I offer ten practical creative discipline tools. They do not need to be adopted together: pick one or two to try in your own family and see what works in your own circumstances. The aims of the tools are to communicate positive values to children, and to decrease family conflict.

Tool 1: Question the reason behind behaviour

We have two ears and one mouth so that we can listen more than we talk.

EPICTETUS

View difficult behaviour as a puzzle and try to find clues for why children have made those choices. What is the motive or intention behind the behaviour? All behaviour is a form of communication. Consider the trigger: what happened immediately before?

Looking for reasons behind behaviour is a very helpful starting point for creative discipline. This 'inward' tool for adults creates a moment of pause: we step back and look objectively at an issue or situation, then respond with more presence and knowledge. This helps us avoid an authoritarian reaction or responding in anger. (Of course we need to react immediately if a situation is dangerous.)

We can also usefully consider the question 'Why?' after an event, or about ongoing and repeated behaviour.

* Does the behaviour indicate an unmet need?
* What is the lesson or value this child needs to learn?
* Could there be a clash between our parenting style or habits and the new needs of this developing child?

At times of family conflict, be brave and ponder:

* Is the issue important?
* Are my expectations realistic given this child's stage of development?
* Is the child's request fair?
* Are my requests fair?
* Are my parenting boundaries fair?
* Is my communication style productive?

Voice of the Author: Lou

My son once queried the true origin of my grumpy behaviour with him, asking, 'What's really going on for you, Mum?'

He was right: I was stressed about something else, which was increasing my bad mood with him.

It is worth thinking about what lies behind our own behaviour as well as the reasons for our children's behaviour!

Consider physical and emotional needs

When you look behind behaviour to ask the reasons why children are making certain choices, it is always worth consciously considering physical and emotional needs. We tend to do this with very young children but can forget it as children grow older, despite physical needs still having a strong impact on behaviour. Children aged 7 to 12 often cannot connect bodily feelings to causes without our prompting.

Consider your children's daily rhythms for:

* sleep
* rest
* meals
* drinks and snacks
* movement
* creativity
* connection times with loving adults

When life is too hurried, daily needs may be compromised, and difficult behaviour increases. Does your family life need to slow down a little and return to healthy rhythms?

Learning values

Often the reason challenging behaviour occurs is that children are still learning a particular value or gaining understanding. Becoming aware of this can help us facilitate that learning with clear communication and loving but firm boundaries.

For example, children aged 7 to 12 are learning:

Delayed gratification: sometimes I need to learn to be patient about the fulfilment of my requests

Empathy: how to step into another's shoes and consider their experience of a situation, which may be different to my own experience

Respect: I need to treat others as I would like to be treated, recognising and respecting that every person wishes to feel happy, loved and safe

Responsibility: my actions create effects and it is kind to make amends if another person is hurt by my actions or words

Teamwork: we are all part of a family team and being helpful creates positive emotions in others, and enjoyable outcomes.

Gently question children

As well as contemplating the reasons behind children's behaviour, I recommend sometimes stopping and asking the children directly. The answer may confirm your own thoughts, or lead you in new directions. Children in the middle years of childhood are developing their capacity to describe feelings and thoughts, and it is worth investing in these new skills.

In a supportive and non-confrontational voice, enquire into the child's world, trying to be genuinely open to hearing all possible answers. Ask questions that start with 'Why...?'. For example, try 'Why are you fighting?' rather than 'Stop fighting!' Try 'Why are you sad?' rather than 'Stop crying!' Each 'Why...?' question can develop children's skills of processing thoughts and emotions into words, and can lead to parents' deeper understanding. Each one can increase our capacity to impart values and guide towards solutions.

In a school where I worked, one boy was avoiding physical activity in a sports class. No amount of coaxing or instructing brought him closer to the game. We interpreted this as rebellion: he was being deliberately oppositional.

But then I asked, 'Why don't you want to join in?'

His quiet response was, 'Because I'm not good at it.'

Sometimes the reason behind refusal is not rebellion but insecurity. This tells us that what the child requires is not chastisement but encouragement.

At times neither children nor adults will be able to point to any reasons behind behaviour, but looking for them is still a very useful first tool.

Tool 2: Transform the word 'no'

Parents tell me that this creative discipline tool has the most positive effect on family harmony.

Often, the emotion lying behind family conflict is a child's disappointment when adults thwart their requests or intentions. Children feel hurt and excluded when the word 'No' is used repeatedly: when they are often denied a request. In the middle years, children are planning their day, thinking up new ideas, and asking for responsibilities. Continued requests are part of children finding new interests, developing life skills and managing time. How do we respond to all these requests so that children feel heard, while adults still hold firm boundaries, keeping children and the family secure, safe and organised?

I suggest trying the alternatives below to stating a simple 'No'. The idea of this tool is not to simply say 'Yes' to everything, giving in to the child and overriding others' needs. It is to create win–win scenarios for the happiness of all.

If at all possible, I recommend trying to say 'Yes' when children request a creative endeavour. Facilitate their best impulses. However, the timing, materials or location may require change.

Of course sometimes adults have to give a simple 'No' to children: there is no adequate time, or the activity doesn't align with family values, or is unsafe or unhealthy or creates disruption for others. But if we reduce the instances of a simple 'No', we can make a big difference to how children experience the family, and this can dramatically reduce conflict and distress.

'Yes, later...'

Children often make requests at moments when we as parents have little spare time. Rather than responding with a simple 'No' and cutting off the child's impulse, try saying 'Yes!' and simply state a suitable time for the activity in the future:

* 'Yes, you can bake a cake on Sunday – we will be visiting Nannie. Write "Bake" on the calendar as a reminder.'
* 'Yes, I'll help you find the Lego pieces after dinner, sort the pieces you can find by yourself for now.'
* 'Yes, you could have walkie-talkies for Christmas! I'll write it on my possible presents list.'
* 'Yes, when you are [certain age] you can have a [request] the same as your sister.'

'No' will be felt by children as a deflating and disappointing response, signifying refusal and an end to their hopes and plans. If you instead start with 'Yes...' and clarify when the request fits into family schedules, children feel heard and supported. They can then practise delayed gratification.

'Yes, later...' works best when we are careful with wording. The emotional impact for the child is very different if we say 'Yes...' then state when the 'yes' will apply, rather than saying 'No, but...'. An answer such as 'No, but we could do it on Monday' might seem to the adult to be saying the same thing, but it will feel deflating to children, who hear the 'No' first.

Sometimes it helps to explain the reason why it's not possible to meet the request right now, especially in a way that helps children empathise.

* 'If I finish making tea now, I can settle and focus with you later.'
* 'I'd like to be on time for our appointment. Keeping other people waiting creates problems for them.'

Children between 7 and 12 are gaining an understanding of time, which means the tool of specifying a later time often works more easily for them than for younger ones. Children of this age also enjoy the written word: write the activity or request on the calendar or on a piece of paper as a reminder. Then make sure the promised time is adhered to!

Rhythms

Limits on certain kinds of food or screen time are necessary but can lead to family conflict. This is less likely, though, if the limited activities or food choices are part of a predictable rhythm. A rhythm also means parents can avoid constantly saying 'No'. Instead they refer to the usual time when the request is granted.

* 'Yes, you can watch it on Saturday!'
* 'Yes, you can choose it for your Friday treat!'

Mention the family value to reinforce and explain your decision. This creates a sense of fairness.

* 'Real bodies like real food.'
* 'We don't have screen time during the week because brain patterns fire up when children create and move.'

These sorts of responses may not stop children complaining in the moment, but do help them understand the rhythm and the reasons. Parents report to me that they overhear their children repeating these kinds of messages about values to their friends.

Alternative suggestions

If a request does not align with family values, try suggesting a healthier, safer or more respectful alternative.

* ✳ 'Yes, let's create our super ice lollies at home rather than buy these artificial ones. Real bodies like real foods!'
* ✳ 'Yes, play ball against the other wall, further away from the lounge, then the noise is not bothering Mum.'

This kind of solution transforms a 'No' to a 'Yes' without parents letting go of family values or putting up with behaviour that impacts negatively on themselves or others. It involves empathising with the children's desire or intention but finding another way of fulfilling it.

Responding with this kind of win–win answer rather than 'No' lets children know that their impulses are heard and understood.

Voice of a Parent: Daniel

Rather than continually saying 'No' due to our busy schedules, the creative discipline tool of saying 'Yes...' and suggesting a suitable time or an alternative activity worked straight away. And without questioning from my children – that was the impressive bit.

No means no

At times, there is no possible alternative time or activity. Or a child has not listened to our 'Yes, later...' response. Sometimes we need to say 'No'. When these occasions arise, give a reason, so that your 'No' seems fair rather than random, and you are reinforcing a family value. These occasions are made easier for children if they know you do say 'Yes' when you can.

If the response to your 'No' is children withdrawing or being defiant, repeat the reason why the request isn't possible, and communicate that you've heard and have empathy for the child or the other people involved. Then move on.

* ✳ 'I know you'd love to play music again, but Nannie is visiting and she has a headache. Come and help us finish the puzzle – we need your brain power!'

Tool 3: Use positive communication

Parents' communication style can either escalate conflict or defuse it. Our voice, tone, language and manner will increase defensiveness and withdrawal or build a bridge to impart and reinforce values.

Remember that discipline is about teaching. It's not easy, but when behaviour is a problem, we need to find a way of talking that lets children learn.

Staying positive

Remember 'You can catch more flies with honey than vinegar.'

This sentiment is also the moral of Aesop's fable 'The North Wind and the Sun', which is often told to 8 year olds in the Steiner-Waldorf curriculum. In the story, the north wind and the sun make a bet that they will be first to strip a traveller of his coat. The wind blows and blows to lift the coat off, but the traveller only wraps it more tightly around his body. Then the sun shines warmly and the traveller takes off his coat.

As parents, we will have more effect if we are warm like the sun than if we blow harsh and hard like the wind.

Tips for positive communication

* Little eye contact and a quiet voice may de-escalate a situation, and allow the value underlying our discipline to be heard.
* Use a low, but assertive and serious voice.
* Talk to children away from a public arena: take them out of the social space before you discipline.
* Use 'I' statements rather than 'You' statements. 'I cannot let anyone be unsafe.' 'I do not want to get a headache from the noise.'
* If children say, 'You are not the boss of me!' Reply, 'I am the boss of ensuring safety and kindness and healthy bodies.'
* Discuss values more fully later, out of the heat of the moment.
* Speak from the heart, especially if there is a deeply felt value at stake.
* Label the behaviour and its effects on others rather than

labelling the child. Say 'Loud voices create headaches!' rather than 'You are such a loud child!'
* Use short sentences with one or two key value words: fewer words can be more powerful and can reduce power struggles.
* Avoid pleading and coaxing.

Look at this list and choose a couple of points to work on this week. We develop new communication skills over time.

Occasionally, children require a stern facial expression and sharp tone when they've dramatically or knowingly overstepped a boundary. But this will be far more effective if we are not stern, angry and shouting – blowing hard like the wind – most of the time.

State the solution not the problem

Use a positive verb. 'Start sharing, let's get a timer' highlights the positive verb 'sharing', whereas 'Stop arguing!' gives emphasis to the negative verb 'argue'. Try 'Talk quietly' rather than 'Stop shouting'. 'Can I hear your lovely manners?' rather than 'Don't be rude'.

Children are much more likely to follow an adult's instruction and much less likely to be defensive if the request seems like guidance and not criticism. Steer children towards the solution: this is my most successful positive communication tool.

Interestingly, when we state the problem, children's unconscious minds may skip the words, 'don't' and 'stop' and 'no' and instead just focus on the action that you wish to change. I once heard a story from an outdoor education teacher. Taking students mountain biking, he had to warn them about certain parts of the path. Over time it became apparent that if he shouted 'Watch out for the trees!' children would have collisions with trees. But when he used the solution-based wording 'Make sure you stay on on the path!' the accidents reduced. He was stating the positive action: the students' minds could focus on 'path' rather than 'trees' – the solution not the problem.

Foster empathy

Appeal to children's empathy when you make requests. This is part of letting them know why a different behaviour is required. For example:

* To encourage sharing: 'The toy will be safe if you both use a timer and take turns, and Nannie's money will not be wasted.'
* To ask for quiet: 'I am starting to get a headache, thank you for lowering your voices.'
* To foster empathy: 'Think with your heart…' I use this with children often and it is amazing to see their responses.

Tool 4: Redirection

Redirection is responding to behaviour that is inappropriate to the location and suggesting where else or how else that behaviour might be possible. It means saying 'You can do that over here instead' rather than saying 'Don't do that.' Or redirection can also be about giving children a completely new activity. For minor issues, or growing tension, redirect their energy by saying 'Let's do this instead!' rather than simply 'Don't do that'.

When children constantly feel told off and reprimanded, or as though they can't move forward with their own activities and plans, conflict increases, as do defiance, avoidance and withdrawal. Redirection avoids telling off. Instead it looks for what is positive in children's behaviour and lets that positive impulse be expressed without family values being breached or other people being inconvenienced.

Redirection recognises that most of children's behaviour is innocently motivated, it just isn't happening in the right place or time. It is my most commonly used creative discipline tool.

Redirect to a new location

If children are being too noisy at a social event, encourage them to play outside, or suggest an inside game of hide and seek. Explain that the change is so their play doesn't add to adult headaches.

If creative play or a building project is taking over the dining room table, rather than packing up the play at the next meal time, set up a folding table for one night, so the building project can be finished but the family meal is also possible.

Redirect to a new activity

If moods are becoming frayed, or siblings are arguing, or if children are overtired or too energetic, step in before tensions grow and conflicts begin. Redirect children to a new activity, or a new environment that will be better suited to the needs of the moment. Suggest listening to stories, for example. Going for a walk or a bike ride can also change the mood. Invite children to help cook a snack. A simple change of scenery or activity often works wonders when there is mounting tension.

Ask children to think of redirection solutions

Explain to children how their behaviour is affecting others so that they can empathise. Then encourage them to use their problem-solving skills and come up with win–win solutions. This promotes the possibility of self-redirection over time – perhaps in future you won't need to intervene.

* 'You want… Your sister wants… How can you both be happy, any ideas…?'
* 'How can Nannie not get a headache and you all still play?'

Tool 5: The power of positive reinforcement

Be on the alert for key family values to acknowledge and praise. Praise is far more effective at changing behaviour than criticism. If the issue you most need to tackle is sibling fights or rude voices, look out for moments when siblings play or talk together positively and give encouragement when it happens. When children use 'please' and 'thank you', say 'Wonderful manners!'. Positive reinforcement creates a feeling of connection and warmth.

Tips for Positive Reinforcement

* Bedtime is a great moment to remember a kind event from the day with a quiet word of encouragement.
* Avoid overpraising or this tool loses its value. Choose particular positive behaviours to highlight.

✳ Label the behaviour and not the child. 'Playing together, happy days – high five!' rather than 'You're such good children when you play nicely.'

✳ Saying thank you can be a positive reinforcement for kind actions and words: 'Thank you for using quiet voices, my headache has gone.' 'Thank you for helping with tea, I couldn't have made it so delicious without you.'

✳ Describe the positive feelings of others. 'I could see your sister felt really proud when you joined in with her friends.'

✳ Positive reinforcement is about acknowledgement not rewards. Giving material rewards for observing family values takes emphasis away from the value itself – children will focus instead on the reward.

Voice of a 10 Year Old: Allison

We have a 'kindness jar' in our house. If my parents spot a kind act they write it down on a piece of paper and place the note in the kindness jar. If we clean up without being asked, help each other out or ask before borrowing something, it is noted down. On Sundays we pick pieces of paper out of the jar to read together.

Tool 6: Storytelling

Children aged 7 to 12 are very responsive to stories. Storytelling can be a great route to learning. If a child is displaying a tricky behaviour, later, when things are quiet, try sharing a story of how you struggled with the same impulse, and conclude with the solutions you learnt over time. When you share personal stories, children feel accepted and understood. Stories can inspire children much more effectively than instructions, and allow children to see their own behaviour from the outside rather than just responding defensively.

Stories can be useful for teaching children life lessons without being explicit or sounding overly authoritarian. Lessons such as delayed gratification, how to be a good sport, or how to use assertive words can all be woven into story time, either through parents' own stories or appropriate chapter books.

I wear a silver necklace with bars that spell out seven key values: respect, strength, kindness, truth, courage, trust and love. Children aged 9 and 10 often ask about my necklace. I read each word, then relate it to a personal story. They listen so intently you could hear a pin drop.

Tool 7: Humour

Rather than nagging, pleading and shouting, humour can deflate conflicts and reinforce family values.

My husband has a 'magic claw': he moves his hand in a pinching motion and chases my daughter to bed! She moves fast, so as not to be tickled.

Try saying the opposite of what you want, rather than nagging, for humorous effect: 'Whatever you do, do not clear the dishwasher. I'd like to eat off dirty plates all week please!'

Sometimes when you could get offended, a comical response will defuse the situation. When a mother explained to me that her 10 year old had upset her by saying she had 'Miss Trunchbull boobs', I suggested playfully joking with the child in return by replying, 'They were the best boobs for breastfeeding you as a baby!'

Voice of a Parent: Daniel

When my children begin to argue, I use playful reprimands to make a point, like insisting, 'Do not share! I will not allow any sharing in this house!' By the time they stop to listen, puzzled, the fighting has stopped too!

Using humour makes everyone feel lighter.

Tool 8: Schedules and the written word

To avoid conflict, middle-years children like decisions to be fair. They also have much greater capacity to read, and to understand charts and schedules. Use the written word to create lists and rosters, which will ensure tasks are fairly shared and decisions fully understood.

The front seat of the car was a big arguing point for my two children. To make it fair, they devised a roster, placed it on the fridge and checked it daily. Using the written word, they independently found a solution to the conflict.

Family meetings

The middle years of childhood are an ideal time to hold 'family meetings', which can be fun while connecting everyone in the family. Family meetings can help the household feel more democratic – they give everyone a chance to be heard on family matters.

Decide on the timing of your meetings: once a month or fortnightly? Write them on the calendar.

Family meetings can include:

* a once-in-a-while food to share – bring out the chocolate!
* deciding on the venue for the next family outing (perhaps choose from a suggestion jar filled with everyone's wishes).
* discussing and settling on family values. Involve children in talking about what makes a 'happy home'. Write out the list of family values, and ask children to help with the lettering and decoration.
* mentioning acts of kindness and other behaviour that could be positively reinforced.
* offering each family member a 'work in progress' – some kind of change that person could make in how they behave at home or a habit they could break or become aware of. This can be done in a jovial manner. Check in with each person's progress at the next family meeting.
* particular topics often arise naturally for discussion during family meetings.

Voice of a Parent: Chloe

After repeated hurtful exchanges between my two children, I wrote out a short list of key values and placed them on the fridge. I found my son reading each word the next morning. Occasionally I'll refer to the list and praise recent positive interactions.

Tool 9: The power of choice

Children aged 7 to 12 are increasingly independent. Conflicts and power struggles will arise when children feel overly controlled. When children of this age are unable to make any of their own choices, they feel powerless. This will happen when parents have an authoritarian approach: 'Do as you are told!'

In contrast, a passive parenting approach provides too many open-ended choices, for example: 'What would you like to eat…'.

Instead of giving no choice or allowing every option, creative discipline offers choices within the parent's boundaries. I'd advise usually giving two or three specific options.

For example, when children are refusing to go to bed, ask, 'How would you like to be put to bed now: reading, massage or chats?'

When children are refusing to complete chores: 'You decide: a weekly roster, one week on and one week off, or a roster for alternate days with your sister?'

If conflicts arise, ask for the child's opinion, and provide limited choices. The idea is that parents hold the boundary, but there is limited freedom and responsibility for children within that. Giving this level of choice decreases battles of wills. However, sometimes parents need to state, 'It is not a choice: bedtime!'

Voice of a Parent: Georgia

This morning, I simply said to my son, 'Get ready now, or play with the Lego for one more minute and then get ready really quickly for school.' I was amazed that he played for a minute and then put his shoes on. It does work to give a choice.

Tool 10: Natural consequence and quiet removal

If we try the creative discipline tools above, and give clear guidance, yet children continue breaking a value by being unsafe, unkind or unhealthy, how do we communicate that we are serious? How do we maintain that value? What happens when children are simply not listening?

We give a 'last chance' to self-regulate behaviour, warning that there is going to be a natural consequence to the behaviour or there will be quiet removal. We tell children they are making a choice. In this way, the child 'chooses' the natural consequence or quiet removal. It is not simply enforced by the parent.

Natural consequences

A natural consequence needs to make sense to the situation. The consequence ideally flows from repairing the value that has been broken. If children won't eat a balanced diet, then perhaps their next once-in-a-while food will need to wait. If the technology contract is ignored, technology time later in the week is taken away, so this keeps life in balance.

* 'Eat your once-in-a-while food today and you'll miss it on Saturday: your choice to keep your body in a healthy balance.'
* 'Dress quickly and we have time for hopscotch before school: your choice.'
* 'Share the toys or I'll put them away to prevent breaking when arguing, which one? Your choice.'
* 'Get ready for bed now, or there will be no time for our story or chat: your choice. You need to fill your sleep tank and be healthy!'

My husband would say, 'Choose your poison!' this was his signal that a consequence was coming. The saying meant, 'This is your last chance to change.'

Children need to understand that behaviour has causes and effects in order for a consequence to be effective. In their middle years, children are old enough to make these connections.

Outside the heat of the moment, it is possible for children to come up with what they think are fair natural consequences for breaking different sorts of values. This kind of discussion could happen during a family meeting.

The quiet removal

If the chance to behave in line with values is ignored, and a situation continues to be unsafe or unkind, then a removal is necessary to create a firm boundary. Depending on the behaviour, the strategy of quiet removal can involve removing an object or yourself or the child. This tool is more powerful if the final boundary is presented as a choice: the child can realign to family values or experience a removal. At this point, children often choose the appropriate way to behave.

Here are examples of presenting removal as a choice:

* 'Kick the ball at the end of the garden away from windows or I'll take it away, your choice.'
* 'Use the timer to share, or I'll remove the toy so it doesn't get broken, your choice.'
* 'Play cards without cheating, so it is fun for everyone, or I'm going to wash up.'

If the choice to change behaviour is ignored, then a firm and quiet removal is now required to maintain the boundary.

Removing an object: take the ball if children are still kicking close to the window; take the toy that is still being fought over and may be broken.

Remove yourself: walk away from the game of cards if a child continually cheats.

Remove the child: walk the child away from a playground game if it has changed to rough play.

When you remove an object, yourself or the child, I recommend doing it silently: it is in these moments that we usually regret our harsh words! Staying silent is powerful; actions speak louder than words.

In circumstances where boundaries and values are disrespected, adults need to create a void to make a point. If children say they will change their ways, while a removal is occurring, give them one last chance. If the inappropriate behaviour continues, resume the quiet removal.

Classroom minutes

In my classroom, if children distract the class or myself on purpose, I say they are taking away other people's minutes, and I will take the time back.

This is a natural and fair consequence. I give a warning that I am watching to see if anyone takes away time and makes other children sit and wait. I reiterate it is not fair to take others' time; I am the keeper of time and I will make sure the minutes are given back to the classroom with a chore at break time.

Rarely do I need to follow through; the warning is enough, especially if I take out a pen and pad to note down any taken minutes and a name.

Taking a break

A child could be asked to take a break or have some chill-out time, especially if the issue you face is sibling squabbles. This strategy contrasts with 'time out', which often creates a defensive, withdrawn, angry energy, and can at times lead to destruction in the room when pent-up emotions boil over.

Later, after the heat of the moment, go to the child who has taken a break and speak quietly, labelling the broken value and asking for a solution, or for ideas about what might make amends.

Remember that there may be two sides to any sibling squabbles. There is more on this in Chapter 10, 'Answers to Common Parent Questions'.

Quiet word

For more serious matters, such as if a child has been distressing or hurting others, use a firm tone and ask to see the child in a short period of time.

Your manner will make it clear that you are feeling disappointed because a value has been broken. Sometimes a child needs to feel a void before they naturally reflect and feel remorse for a broken value. Every child and person desires deep down to belong, and to return to harmony with the family.

Once it is time to talk, use a serious facial expression, silent pauses and a few key words. This will express the message louder than shouting. The child needs to understand the effect of their behaviour, to connect emotionally to the situation and the outcome. For example, 'One main role of parents is to teach children not to hurt others. I will not accept hitting on any level.'

Using only a small number of words means you are much more likely to be understood. Speak in short sentences, highlight values, emphasise keywords: 'kind', 'unsafe'. Once the key message is absorbed, reaffirm your belief in the child to act in a safe or kind way in the future.

Making amends

When you are having a quiet word, children may naturally apologise. I'd advise against forcing apologies. Instead, ask the child to suggest things to do that would repair hurt feelings or wipe the slate clean. I often suggest that the child reassures the person who has been hurt that the behaviour will not happen again. A caring act is likely to be more in harmony with the family value of kindness than a forced apology.

If children refuse an act of amends you've suggested, you can personally role model the kind act, and encourage them to make amends in the future. They may be feeling shameful, and require reassurance that it is OK to make mistakes, but important to make up afterwards. Alternatively, they may feel that it is not all their fault, and there are two sides to the story. However, children usually like to make amends to create a clean slate.

Making amends is more powerful than punishment.

During a family meeting, everyone can contribute to a list of actions that might help repair the situation after a value has been broken. Ask: 'What makes you happy if you're sad?'

Some examples of what we can do for someone who is upset:

* pour them a glass of water
* bring a comfort blanket
* complete a chore on their behalf
* give a hug
* read or share a book
* listen to some music together
* tell a joke

The list is endless!

A kind act replaces unkind behaviour and a new beginning is established.

Voice of a 10 Year Old: Alison

If I do something wrong, my parents tell me the mistake, and tell me not do it again, that it is not 'right'. They say it is OK to do it once, but try not to do it a second time. Mistakes are what you can learn from. If I do make a mistake twice, my consequence is usually an extra chore, to give back and help my family.

Using the 10 Creative Discipline Tools

The ten tools are not presented as a set formula. If a discipline issue arises, look through the tools outlined above to find ideas. Communication is always vital.

Don't feel overwhelmed by having a number of parenting tools to try. Perhaps choose one tool to practise, and then another a week later, until a creative discipline approach starts to feel natural. See what works and what doesn't: every child and family situation is unique.

There is no right and wrong. Occasionally authoritarian and passive reactions are required, but when we use the creative discipline tools most of the time, adults and children tend to thrive.

The model of discipline and family values instilled during middle childhood forms a basis for the teenage years. Parents need to focus time and energy on supporting children during middle childhood, and providing loving boundaries and guidance. The long-term aim is to teach children to regulate their own behaviour even when we are not there. Mistakes are helpful lessons along the way for both parent and child.

Life will be full of ups and downs. I certainly did not practise all the above strategies with my own children. Remember that almost all difficult situations can be healed if there is a genuine intent to rebuild connection, and this will help carry you through the teenage years.

Voice of the Author: Lou

My 16-year-old daughter recently enquired, 'How do you think you're going as a parent, Mum?' (It's unusual to have a mum who is a parenting author!)

I answered honestly, 'If I had my time again, I would definitely change certain situations, and act differently. But I believe I've been "good enough".'

Parenting is not about perfection, it's about living, and life is ever-changing. As the saying goes, the journey is more important than the destination. Human beings are always in training.

Striving for your family values is a meaningful life. Parents are the gatekeepers, ensuring which values will evolve and pass to future generations.

In Brief: 'That's Unfair!' – Creative Discipline Ideas

* Discipline is a positive word. It means training in values, to develop a happy, healthy and meaningful life.
* Look at the reasons behind behaviour: look within, and question the child too.
* Transform the word 'No' while still holding boundaries when children make requests. This will reduce daily conflict.
* Use fewer words in a calm, quiet and serious voice. This de-escalates conflict.
* Try humour at times.
* Tell personal stories after the event.
* Where different people's needs are in conflict, redirect children so their impulses can be followed without disrupting others. Ask children for their own win–win solutions too.
* Positively reinforce behaviour you wish to see again.
* Use choice, to teach self-regulation over time and to avoid power struggles. Choices happen within boundaries that are given by parents, referring to the family's key values.
* Children's behaviour choices may lead to a natural consequence

or quiet removal. Give a warning before this last, firm approach is implemented.

* If a natural consequence or quiet removal is required, speak of the broken value and suggest an act that could 'make amends' and clean the slate.

* Life is a journey. Everyone will make mistakes – children and parents. Rebuild a bridge of connection and understanding where possible. It will need rebuilding many times, but often becomes stronger with each rebuild!

CHAPTER TEN
Answers to Common Parent Questions

We can have the best values and parenting models in the world, but sometimes we just need practical suggestions to deal with everyday challenges, and to hear what works for others.

With that in mind, for this chapter I have compiled the most common parent questions about 7 to 12 year olds that I have encountered throughout my years as a teacher, parent and presenter. Metaphorically, 'It takes a village to raise a child'. But nowadays ideas are passed on through reading books, listening to talks, and observing and sharing with others, for example with other school parents and friends. There are many parent voices within this chapter, so as to provide a village in a book. Choose suggestions and voices which resonate with your truth, as every family dynamic is unique.

Question 1
When is the appropriate age for children to start contributing to family chores?

Children under 7 'play' at chores. They have a strong impulse to imitate and imagine, that is, to copy adult carers. So while you are sweeping, they may want to sweep too with an appropriately sized brush, but usually they are copying a motion rather than fully understanding the purpose of the activity.

In contrast, children from 7 to 12 years can start to complete chores independently, and this increases their self-sufficiency and confidence, which is important for the 9-year crossing and beyond. After 9 years is an excellent time for introducing independent chores that contribute to family life. Common tasks include: cooking and laying the table, loading and unloading the dishwasher, washing up, making the bed and tidying bedrooms.

Try to assign tasks which fit naturally into the other rhythms of family life. I talked with a parent whose morning school routine was frazzled. We worked out that this was due to her having to constantly remind her children to unload the dishwasher before breakfast. The timing was clearly not working, but this was easily solved by shifting the dishwashing time to after school, so the unloading task happened just before the evening meal when the children were more alert and the family schedule wasn't as tight. They could also chat to their parent in the kitchen while unloading; children often like company while completing chores.

Avoid labelling children in an angry moment, for example, calling them lazy when they are resisting helping with chores. These labels stay with children and can work against them joining in later. It is important to keep encouraging and providing opportunities to participate in family chores, and to stay firm at times. Create a fun family rhythm for chores, so that tasks are less burdensome and more enjoyable for all involved!

Completing family chores together

Children during the middle years are naturally family-orientated, so now is the time to get them used to completing family tasks together in a fun and connecting way. Rather than nagging them to pick up a sock, try to create regular daily and weekly rhythms for chores so that they become automatic and supportive rather than just burdensome. Regular rhythms for chores reduce the need to constantly remind children about them. Working together and equally allows everyone to feel they are part of a family team. Children often enjoy adult company or listening to music while cleaning their rooms. The list of chores to be done can also be created by the whole family together. If you have family meetings, the question of what needs to be done can be discussed in the meeting.

Two popular ideas for bringing predictability and enjoyment to family life are a kitchen-helper roster and a Saturday cleaning hour.

Kitchen helper

Create a kitchen-helper roster. The kitchen helper chooses the meal (if time allows), assists with the food preparation and cooking, lays the table and helps to wash up. This is a wonderful way to involve children in their middle years in family life, creating a sense of belonging, importance and contribution. They also learn vital cooking skills and care for their home and for daily rituals.

Start every meal with a big thank you to the chefs!

Voice of a Parent: Chloe

My partner and I have four children between us, ranging from age 7 to 14. Each child has a designated weekly night to be a 'kitchen helper'.

We give a lot of thanks at our dinner table to the chefs: children appreciate gratitude and being the centre of attention.

Saturday cleaning hour

Set aside an hour on the weekend for the whole family to clean together. Everyone in the house commits to tidying or cleaning at the same time. Play music while you clean. You are teaching children that many hands make light work: when all family members pitch in together it creates a buoyant and friendly atmosphere. Children could tidy bedrooms during this time, while adults are doing other tidying and sorting.

Once the chores are completed, perhaps turn to a family pizza-making, board game or movie night. I have found there is a natural progression to settling down and enjoying the late afternoon and evening together once the house is organised and clean.

> ### Tip - Chores Can Be Fun!
>
> Play beat the hourglass or timer while completing family chores. This will motivate everyone to keep up their pace, and it will feel like a game.

Remind with humour rather than nagging

In my home, if the dishwasher is full of clean plates at the evening meal time, because no one has unloaded it, I place the dinner on the table and say, 'Interesting! How are we going to eat this?'

This is also an example of natural consequences: if we don't put plates away they are not there to eat from next time.

If my husband has to ask our teenagers to empty the dishwasher more than twice, he pretends to sit on them, saying, 'Sorry, I thought you were at the dishwasher!' They move quickly!

> ### Voice of a Parent: Georgia
>
> My children now know to always take their dishes to the sink and put their dirty clothes in the laundry basket: this is just part of everyday family life. Initially it required constant prompting, which we tried to do in a fun way, but now they just do it without thinking about it.
>
> They display pride in their chores.

Question 2

Is it advisable to pay children for jobs around the house and to give pocket money?

In my home, we decided that everyday chores are simply part of family life, and they were unpaid. We were creating a family 'team' ethos. If a child naturally enjoys cooking, for example, financial reward can actually devalue the spontaneous appeal of the activity.

I also think it is important that parents can ask for a helpful hand from time to time without there being any question of payment. This encourages kindness.

However, children 9 years old and older enjoy completing extra tasks for a small monetary gain, and this can become a useful lesson in earning and saving. Parents might choose to offer money for chores such as dusting, vacuuming, extra loads and unloads of the dishwasher, gardening and cleaning windows and cars.

If you are going to offer money, discuss the rules for how it may be saved and spent. A 10 year old with money to spend may want purchases such as sweets and plastic throw-away toys that conflict with family values, and this is likely to lead to arguments.

My husband set up bank accounts for our children when they turned 12. If chore money was banked and stayed in the account until they turned 18, it was doubled. Our children loved seeing their account money grow. As an accountant, my husband was keen to teach financial literacy and the power over time of regularly saving a little money.

Parents may choose to introduce a monetary reward for complex chores that are an extra contribution, rather than for everyday activities which are naturally part of family life. Otherwise when asked to pick their pyjamas up from the floor, children may respond with, 'What will you pay me to do it?'

Children in the middle years of childhood still need parents' and carers' guidance on spending money. Rather than providing pocket money, it is helpful if we name a specific purpose when giving children some coins, for example Friday lunch money, going out with a friend, or a treat that children may choose for themselves on a particular day of the week. Family values and rules about spending need to be clear and consistent.

Voice of a 10 Year Old: Paula

I make my bed and fold the washing.

Voice of a 12 Year Old: Zac

I do extra chores of weeding and mowing the lawns. I'm saving up for a camera.

Voice of a 10 Year Old: Georgia

I set the dinner table, empty and fill the dishwasher, and make my bed. Sometimes I garden, dust and vacuum when Mum or Dad asks, and I get money each week.

Voice of a 9 Year Old: Ilija

I help with the dishwasher and bins, and tidy my room. I'm doing extra unloads of the dishwasher as I'm saving for an electronic car.

Tip - Jobs Jar

School holidays are a good time for children to do a few extra chores and earn some money. Write all the extra tasks on pieces of paper and place them in a jar to make a lucky dip.

Question 3
What is a helpful response to my child's new attitude?

It can be a shock when children answer back. As parents we may sometimes be surprised by our own strong reaction to this behaviour. We can feel anger that our child is displaying what appears selfish behaviour, and sadness at their detachment from us, and we can even begin to question whether we are ourselves at fault and wonder whether we perhaps deserve this new attitude. 'Attitude' from middle-years children can mean they suddenly feel very different from the children we knew during their younger years.

Voice of a Parent: Mandy

When my 10-year-old son suddenly had an attitude and answered back, I felt it was a reflection on me. I have to admit, at times I felt like a bad parent.

Having attitude

Criticism, disagreements, answering back and the occasional eye-roll are common reactions from 9 years of age. In the middle years of childhood, we all try to move away from the tight hold of our parents and gain more independence. An 'attitude' is a way of expressing resistance and separateness, of perhaps complying physically while showing that your mind is your own. A new sense of individuality leads to attitude, as do stronger emotions, alongside a growing awareness of comparisons with others.

Most parents I meet are rather shocked when first encountering a passive, defiant eye-roll. They feel it is a personal attack. But it is important to pull back, and not overreact in the moment. The eye-roll is often a spontaneous and, at times, unconscious act. The act of rolling eyes upwards, without words, is a way to push back. Children may be pushing back against the instruction, or the word 'No', or the adult's tone or manner. It's important to recognise that 9 to 12 year olds don't yet have the language skills to attempt a negotiation, or feel they may not be successful in it. An eye-roll is used to signify they are doing something under duress.

Parent responses to attitude

As a parent it is important to stay calm. Challenging decisions and trying to negotiate boundaries are common with children of this age, and thus some degree of 'attitude' is normal. But parents and teachers can still moderate children's words, and insist on respectful and kind behaviour overall.

It's not necessary to confront every single instance of attitude head-on. Save your strong responses for the worst instances or for bigger issues. Most instances of attitude just require humour, redirection or a big outpouring of love. Try saying: 'I know I'm annoying!'

Use a light-hearted response, and still draw the line at a negative tone. Try:

* 'I can't hear you!' said with a smile. (This means: 'Say it in a more respectful way if you want me to hear and respond.')

If a child says, 'I don't care … !', reply in a loving tone. Try:

* 'Well I care about you.' This is an example of lovingly reinforcing family values.

If the challenge is more rude or more serious, try calm and firm:

* 'Excuse me?'
* 'Try again!'
* 'Doesn't work.'

These responses assert your parental authority, which is necessary at times, but don't overuse this approach. It is best reserved for when you need to signify that a line of respect has been crossed.

Role-model healthy boundaries. Try:

* 'I don't let anyone talk to me like that: not the bus driver, not colleagues, not Dad. Now try again.'

As well as responding directly to your children's behaviour, take time to consider the trigger point before the 'attitude' response. What is leading to this behaviour? Look again at ideas in Chapter 9 for transforming the answer 'No'. Ask yourself whether the boundary is fair, and whether you are providing a choice. If deemed unfair, your children may be responding out of frustration. By asking ourselves these questions, we meet children in their new stage of development.

Finally, look carefully at your own tone and your own responses to your children and to others. Remember that adults can display attitude too – I know!

Voice of a Parent: Georgia

Tonight when I said it was bedtime, my son responded, 'I don't care!'

I remembered Lou's suggestion and replied, 'Well I really care for you.' I said it very lovingly and my son stopped to take in how much I cared for him. I went on to explain how his body required sleep.

I also allowed him 'one more minute' of reading. I'm amazed that offering even a little more time works: he was settled after the minute.

Voice of a Parent: Chloe

I find it works to playfully imitate my children's tone or look. At times I can make them laugh. But I only use this tool in a playful way – I'm careful not to sound demeaning – I wouldn't use it if the mood was serious, as it could backfire, create anger, and then take more energy to resolve.

If my child's attitude is more serious, I simply state my feelings, without too much emotion: 'I am not enjoying that look.'

Question 4
How can I encourage manners?

Practising manners means giving full attention momentarily to gratefulness and kindness. Manners may appear to be a simple exchange or a mere surface polish to social interaction, but profound and sustaining values underpin the use of phrases like 'please' and 'thank you'. Manners are a vital life skill, and also a tool for good health: expressing gratitude can help alleviate feelings of depression. Manners are also about self-respect: they keep the bar high in life. So good manners are a rich gift we can offer our children.

Manners become second nature if there is regular loving practice and prompting during the middle years. Take advantage of natural daily opportunities to encourage the words 'please' and 'thank you'. For example:

* At meal times, rather than handing your child their plate, hold it and wait expectantly until they say 'thank you'.
* Wait with raised eyebrows for a 'please' before you grant a request.
* When picking children up from visits to other homes, pause in a meaningful way or give an expectant look until they say 'thank you' to their hosts. This will work best if you have discussed beforehand what you are expecting and practised a form of words. Or whisper 'Thank you for having me' for your children to repeat out loud.

Encouraging manners can help soften children's 'attitude' at times: attitude is hard to maintain when we are grateful for what we have and for what others give.

Voice of a Parent: Georgia

My children seem well received in other homes, so I know they have absorbed some manners.

Manners open doors

Once children are in their teenage years and venturing out into the world, the importance of manners becomes more evident. I often say to my children, 'Manners matter!' and 'Manners open doors!'

Recently, my daughter was anxious before her first day of work experience. I said, 'Smile, use your manners, and all will be fine.' And it was: she was offered ongoing work within three days.

Question 5
What is a positive approach to arguments between siblings?

In adult life there is a basic assumption that we try to act with civility towards each other, and that our interactions will take place on a basis of respect. Sometimes we forget that we all had to learn how to get along with other people despite having differing opinions. Getting along involves the art of conflict resolution. What are the principles and strategies of conflict resolution?

* Taking it in turns to talk, communication.
* Hearing the other person's side, listening.
* Stepping into the other person's shoes, empathising.
* Agreeing to disagree, letting it go.
* Finding a win–win solution or compromise.

The years between age 7 and 12 are the perfect stage of development to introduce positive and constructive conflict-resolution skills. Children in their middle years can recognise cause and effect (though usually only after the event!), so they understand the nature of consequences. They also have a greater capacity for empathy than young children; they can start to step outside themselves and feel with another person. With their growing sense of 'aloneness' comes an opposite need to get along with their peers, and to share. With these new attributes, they are able to enter into more active conflict resolution, often assisted by an adult at first.

After an argument

The capacities of middle-years children can become evident after an argument between siblings or friends. Wait until things have quietened down, and then put the two children back together. Create the space to reflect and see the other's side. What happens? Surprisingly often you will witness a resolution, apologies and the happiness of renewed closeness.

If one child is crying, the other child may quickly realise their part in the emotion. If the altercation is one-sided, suggest a natural apology or a way to make amends to wipe the slate clean. Always emphasise the possibility of making things right again: say clearly that it is OK to make mistakes, but it is always good to make up.

Most of the time, there are two sides to an altercation. Ask siblings to face each other and share their feelings while you mediate. Possible prompts for the children include:

* 'I didn't like it when…'
* 'It made me feel…'

The idea is that each child in turn hears the other point of view in the conflict, particularly the emotions the other person felt. You as the parent witness the exchange, encourage a solution and reinforce positive values. Aim for a mode of brief, simple prompts, and questions, such as:

* 'Can you think of a solution?'
* 'How could you get along next time?'
* 'Can you think of a way to make amends?'

One child may refuse to meet with the other due to feelings of innocence, embarrassment, or defensiveness, or because they are still too angry. Give them time. There will always need to be time after the argument before real discussion is possible. If you as the parent are able to use a neutral rather than a cross tone, children will usually come together when they're ready, and resolve the conflict.

Note that sometimes we don't need to intervene at all. Ideally, we are moving towards children having the skills and maturity to manage without our intervention. When children argue, allow time to see whether they are able to resolve the conflict themselves. They may independently suggest solutions. Observe and listen first, and only intervene if the tension is increasing and an explosion is imminent.

When you think the issue is minor, instead of entering into conflict resolution, encourage the child who is complaining to find a mode of resilience. Teach them to walk away and find calmness again. Try the phrase: 'Water off a duck's back, shake it off!' It helps if adults playfully model the action.

Tip - Suggest a Break

When siblings are becoming heated, suggest 'special time', which translates as taking a break from each other in different parts of the house. Children can need parents to recommend a break; they may not have the negotiation skills to take themselves off. It is important that taking a break is not presented as a punishment or isolation, but as a helpful strategy they can use to defuse tension.

Foster positive sibling relationships

After the 9-year crossing, children understand that families are for life. Occasionally, I would remind my children of the important value of family, to reinforce their bond. I would say, 'Please try and get along. This is not just for today: you are brother and sister for life!' I would then describe a few scenarios of life events together:

* 'We may spend our birthdays together throughout the years.'
* 'Friends may come and go, but family is for life. How lucky are we?!'
* Remark on the positive nature of siblings with your children. 'How great is it to have someone to play soccer with at home!' I used to say: 'Sibling power!' and give my two children a fist bump!

Tip - Sharing

When siblings need to share, suggest timing turns or creating a roster. Use the games of 'rock, paper, scissors' or 'heads or tails' to see who goes first.

Defuse with humour

Using humour can defuse a developing situation and help prevent an argument. It can also build resilience in your children. Perhaps try accentuating the opposite of what you seek: 'Whatever you do, do not get along! We don't want any family happiness today!'

Voice of a Parent: Michael

I try to be a little lighter, even playful, myself when my children argue. It certainly works at times.

Voice of a Parent: Chloe

When my children argue, I place a drop of lavender oil on my finger and chase them, trying to put a spot of it between their eyebrows to encourage peace and happiness!

Voice of a Parent: Georgia

Recently I heard my friend's final warning to her two arguing children. She calmly said, 'Do you want me to get mad at you?' and 'Can you tell that my voice is changing?' I was surprised that they responded and stopped.

Do no harm

Siblings do not have to be best friends; during the middle years they develop strong peer friendships with children their own age. However, it is important to establish the value in your home of 'Do no harm'. If actions cross the line into being unsafe or harmful, direct parent action is required.

The middle years is a crucial time to curb all sibling hitting. Hitting in anger requires a strong response from you every time: 'It is NOT OK to hit!' After each new incident, replay the lead-up to show how a different solution could have been reached, or to discuss other ways to express the emotions.

If children have a tendency to lash out when they are upset, this often indicates that they lack verbal skills to express how they are feeling. Discuss the consequences of hurting others. Help children feel empathy with those they hit. 'Look at his face, he is sad and does not feel safe. How can you reassure him now that he is safe?' Tell them that it is OK to be angry, to get upset, to be disappointed or frustrated, even bored, but these emotions must be expressed in a safe way.

Encourage children to recognise when their sibling is frustrating them and to say, 'Stop I don't like it!' Suggest they repeat 'Stop!' three times. If the sibling ignores the request, then encourage the frustrated child to find an adult, rather than hit out. Praise your children when they try a new behaviour, when they negotiate verbally rather than physically, and when they listen to the word 'Stop!' from their sibling.

If you have an ongoing issue with hitting, consider creating a marking system on the calendar noting days when anger is not expressed physically. The aim is not to build to a reward, but for the family to recognise and positively reinforce changing behaviour.

Each time a child hits, respond with a firm voice: state the boundary that has been crossed – 'Stop! Everybody has a right to feel safe in our home' – and create a time of reflection, then encourage a kind act to make amends.

Look back at Chapter 7, 'Managing Children's Anger', for more ideas. Be persistent and consistent every time: you are developing emotional skills for life!

Taunting

When hurtful behaviour is not physical but verbal, take the sibling who is being unkind aside. Describe putting others down as a low act, designed to make the others feel small. Insist that the sibling is better than this. Explain that kindness is uplifting.

Limits in action

I have an example of setting limits on physical behaviour from my own family.

My husband is very calm, patient and understanding; however, when my son dragged his sister from the front seat of the car, hurting her, it was necessary to mark a boundary.

My husband took my son's hands and quietly but firmly held them down. My son felt the reprimand. My husband then asked to see him in ten minutes' time. After that ten minutes, he spoke in a firm but fair manner. He said that his first job as a parent was to teach his children to refrain from hurting others, and this lesson was practised with siblings first. He ensured his disappointment was obvious without saying too many words.

After feeling the severity of the situation, our son apologised, and he wrote out a roster for turns in the front seat of the car.

Ask yourself 'why?'

When there is arguing and hurtful behaviour in your family, take time to reflect on the possible causes and reasons. Think about what triggered recent incidents. What else is going on for the children? In family life?

Children are more likely to argue when they are tired or stressed. Fighting with a sibling may mask a deeper issue for a child. Children are also more likely to be fractious when we parents are tired or stressed!

Voice of a Parent: Chloe

I have noticed that when I am tired or stressed, my children seem to fight all the time. It is as if they are aware that I am not present with them, and fighting is an unconscious way to get my attention. When I am present and happy, if they argue it dissipates without so much charge. If I am stressed, run-down, overwhelmed, and my tolerance is low, there is a tendency for moods to snowball.

Voice of an 11 Year Old: Ocea

If I've had a bad day at school, I find everything my sister does annoys me.

My mum tells me to lie on my bed, and she puts a crystal on my chest. She then tells me to breathe, so I can watch the crystal go up and down. It does help.

Question Six
How can I encourage children to tell the truth?

Children sometimes choose self-preservation over integrity: they will try to avoid the consequences of their actions by lying about them. This is understandable – we all recognise the fear of shame or a potential punishment. Yet honesty is one of the highest values in any relationship. Being honest is like having someone else's back: it builds trust. Without trust, there is no relationship. So we need to be truthful, where possible, with children, foster the value of honesty, and reinforce their choices when they are honest with us.

* Talk within the family about honesty and trust. Explain that it is the foundation to all relationships.
* Tell children that there is nothing that cannot be expressed. Ensure that children never have cause to regret telling the truth – that no one feels humiliated for what they confess or reveal.

❋ The story 'The Boy Who Cried Wolf' warns of what can happen when we exploit others' trust.

❋ Say it takes a lot of courage to be honest. Then tell your children you know they have courage.

❋ Ensure that any consequences are reduced when children have the courage to make an honest confession. This shows how much you value honesty.

Question Seven
What is a reasonable response to swearing?

It can be a shock for us to hear our children swear, especially the first time. Children between ages 7 and 12 sometimes play with swear words, trying them out to see an adult's response. Often they won't really understand the full meaning or impact of the words they are using. While there are good reasons to respond firmly to swearing, if we overreact, we may give the words more power than they deserve, a child may feel harshly condemned for copying a peer's words without full understanding, and parents may miss the chance to talk calmly about why it matters that we don't use swear words.

Think about why children shouldn't swear. Rather than just saying that a word is rude, stress the social consequences. If children swear at their friends' houses, other parents can be offended or regard the behaviour as anti-social. Children who swear may not be asked back. It is helpful for children to understand that it is socially inappropriate to swear in the company of adults, teachers, parents and strangers. Avoiding swear words is a common value in society and shows respect for those we are talking to.

Paint a picture for children of the repercussions of swearing. Explain that if the brain gets used to swearing it is hard to stop. It becomes a habit which can lead to social trouble.

If your family has rules about swearing, those rules need to be followed by everyone, parents included. Be a role model yourself: say 'flip' and 'sugar' during trying moments.

> ### Tip - Make Up Funny Words
>
> Make up fun family words such as 'flibber flobber' to use when frustrated.

Question Eight
Is it ever a good idea to get involved in your children's friendships?

There is a difficult but crucial balance to be found here. When your children are struggling with friendship difficulties, it is important not to overreact, or leap in too early with advice or your own interventions. Yet it is also an essential part of our role as parents to notice when our children are distressed, and to take steps if you think children are coming to any physical or emotional harm.

With minor complaints about friendships and peer group, I suggest an attitude of 'less is best': listen, but do not step in, as friendship dynamics do tend to work themselves out in the end. When we as parents become anxious about our children's friendships, or express our own opinions, we may inadvertently magnify and prolong the friendship issues. See the friendship ideas in Chapter 8, 'Suggestions for Anxiety'.

However, if children cry and show other physical signs of distress, ask open-ended questions. Try to gently uncover the root of the friendship anxiety, workshop ideas with your child, and respond. Ask the child's teacher to be on the lookout for any difficulties at school.

It is a delicate balance, but we have to weigh up the severity of the issue and the lasting effect for children.

If you think children may be experiencing emotional or physical bullying it is important to act straight away.

What is bullying?

There is a big difference between the changes and fluctuations in friendship groups and bullying, one-off incidents and bullying, and also between playful teasing and bullying. The word 'bully' is often over-used. We need to make sure we understand what it means, so children are not labelled unnecessarily, and the meaning of the word is not watered-down. Bullying is severe behaviour. Bullying is a repeated pattern of speech or action that specifically aims to hurt someone else, emotionally or physically. If you suspect a behaviour falls into the 'bullying' category, report the incidences to the school and to the relevant teachers straight away. Or, if bullying is occurring outside school, you will need to notify the other child's parents with your concerns in a calm manner, where possible.

Voice of a Parent: Mel

When each of my children started high school at 12, I spoke to them about finding their 'tribe'. I spoke about watching feelings and sensations when around different friends. Did they feel uncomfortable, bored, happy? Their feelings would lead them to the right friendship group.

Be a friendly parent

I strongly recommend being a parent who welcomes your children's friends into your home, speaks to them and picks them up from gatherings. Cook for them. Listen: they may talk about many things in the back of the car. This is your chance to see what is going on in their lives, to understand the world from their varied perspectives.

Question 9

What limits are advisable for children's use of screen technology?

This is a question I am asked often. When is a good age to introduce screen-based media and technology? What limits should we set?

Our children are surrounded by media and technology. Most homes include multiple computers, tablets and phones. I love technology; it helps life in so many ways: seeing and speaking to family overseas, writing books, emailing, storing photos. Computers and phones are wonderful and useful tools.

However, limits are required while growing up (and in adult life too). There are many studies today showing the negative effects on children of too much technology, including decreased attention spans, increased impulsivity, an impact on cognitive function because overstimulation short-circuits the learning process, a decrease in emotional processing along with a decrease in face-to-face social and communication opportunities, and an increase in near-sightedness. I have read that some tech bosses reduce their children's screen time, because they understand the effects.

This is an area where it will be very difficult for children to make an informed and free choice, so we as parents need to come to a conscious decision about when and how to allow technology. Observe your children's moods before, during and after technology use, and that can help guide your decision.

Different families will come to different conclusions. My own children grew up before the huge wave of iPad and phone games. They had limited TV with a rhythm of a Saturday family movie night once older (where we watched many home movies and cooking shows as a family). Two years after the 9-year crossing, we consciously allowed access to an interactive sport and movement game, which the whole family enjoyed together. We played tennis and bowling. We withheld 'shooting' games. With little variety in games, and a firm rhythm of screen time, my children soon got bored with the games and focused on other activities. Now they are in their late teenage years, they use technology in many ways: socially, educationally and for entertainment.

I believe children require education on why we limit use and the effects of technology addiction.

Rather than judge, I aim to highlight the positive rewards gained from limited or no technology use during the middle years of childhood. I am passionate about reading, creative pursuits, especially cooking, movement games and family connection time. All these activities increase when technology has not taken over leisure time.

Setting limits on screen time

Here are some ideas to assist in thinking about and setting limits:

* Delay children's adoption of technology as long as possible. What they do not know about, they will not pester and whine for! They will play and read if they are not overstimulated by screen-based media.
* Children enjoy using tablets as tools, to look up recipes, talk face to face with relatives, explore family photos and create short family videos.
* When introducing technology, start with a simple game or activity that connects to real life. Limit the number of games downloaded on the family tablet: more games means even more stimulation.
* Place the computer in a family area, and insist games are played outside of bedrooms. If adults join in with games or watch movies with children, this increases social interaction. Adults can also discuss plots and characters.
* Create weekly rhythms around technology use. Have limits for when technology will and won't be allowed, and stick to them – to keep life in balance. Specifying that screens will be a weekend-only activity, for example, can be very helpful.
* Don't be afraid to specify the kinds of screen games allowed and the schedules for screen time to fit with your family values.
* Avoiding a judgemental tone, share stories about how addictive screen time can be. Use 'I' statements: 'I am concerned how prolonged screen time effects the brain. I want to look after your brain!'
* Find classic movies: they tend to be less stimulating, and more engaging for the imagination.
* Introduce movies that are wholesome. We played our home-made videos of our children growing up and of yearly family holidays for many years.
* Encourage the joy of cooking by introducing a cooking show.
* Note movie ratings and observe them. Shocking images may disturb 7 to 12 year olds on a deep level.
* When children are going on a sleepover at a friend's house,

check with parents beforehand how much screen time is expected and the particular movies to be shown.

* Temper your own media use around children and avoid it altogether at family times.

* Use a consistent saying, for example, 'Your brain neurons will light up when you creatively think and move!'

* If technology has taken over children's leisure time, create a jar of ideas from Chapter 6 and redirect the child to take a lucky dip to redirect to a real-life activity that requires gross- and fine-motor skills, creative thinking and more.

* Make sure children have access to the wonderful activities suggested throughout this book and plenty of opportunities to connect with adults. Then technology will not leave such a hole in their lives. Children love card games at this age.

Voice of a Parent: Lisa

I have a rule: half an hour of reading, half an hour of craft, half an hour outside and *then* Saturday screen time.

Voice of a Parent: Bruce

We have a rule that there is no screen time in the week. It is so much easier now this blanket rule is in place.

Voice of a Parent: Lulu

I have a rule of no guns or violence in games. I say in an exaggerated way, 'I can't have violence in my house.'

Voice of a Parent: Georgia

I allow my 9 year old a car-racing game and an educational game. Even with this small amount of choice I see the strong allure pulling him. At times, I put a media ban on for a few weeks, when I am aware he is getting more addicted. Today we went for a bike ride instead, and stopped for some bird watching. He loved it!

Voice of the Author: Lou

When my son was 12, he was so keen to have a computer game but I was hesitant about any violence in games. I found a train and plane simulator, where he actually learnt to drive a train. The scenery was true to life. It was quite relaxing!

Question 10

When is a good age to discuss smoking, drinking alcohol and stranger danger?

In my experience it is easier to introduce the topics of smoking and alcohol after the 9-year crossing, between 10 and 12 years. Children at this age tend to be very averse to smoking. Talking naturally about health issues during dinner-time conversations lays the foundation for the teenage years.

The idea is not to lecture but to watch for opportunities to guide and to relay important messages about self-respect and health. Try not to avoid these topics, and notice when they naturally arise during conversations. Messages are absorbed easily at this age and last into the teen years, creating avenues for continued family discussion and guidance.

Stranger danger

Between 9 and 12 years of age, children are likely to seek further independence, such as asking to pop to the shops on short errands or to go on a short bike ride with friends. It is essential that parents speak to children about safety and 'stranger danger'. How can we have these conversations without creating unnecessary fear?

I found it useful to frame my conversations around real-life scenarios. First, it is reassuring to let children know that most people in the world are essentially good and kind, but a few people in the world are not. I reiterated that meeting someone like this was highly unlikely, and would probably never happen, but it is still good to know the following:

* No one will pick you up from school, unless I have told you or the office staff tell you. I will not send someone you do not know to pick you up from school.
* Do not take sweets or lollies from strangers.
* No unknown adult should ask a child to come and help them, for example, to look for their dog.
* If someone tries to take your hand or move you, it is not time to be polite but to scream louder than a lion and run to another adult.
* If you ever feel uncomfortable, go into a shop or a place with other adults.
* Never go into a public toilet on your own.
* Never go up to a stranger's car, or get in, even if they want to show you something inside.

The idea is to inform children about stranger danger, but not to scare them (especially during the 9-year crossing). It is important to always keep children with you, and to repeat this topic when they are spending short periods of time alone.

Now my children are teenagers, I remind them to look after each other, and their friends, and I go through specific scenarios if they are attending a music festival or community event.

In Brief: Answers to Common Parent Questions

* Start a 'kitchen-helper' roster and set aside a family cleaning time each week.
* Extra chores may gain a monetary reward. Help children decide beforehand what to save for.
* Watch for the triggers before an 'attitude' moment and look within.
* Meet a child's attitude with humour and calmness, to make a point and avoid a power struggle.
* Manners matter: play games that teach this value for life.
* Siblings are for life: remind children of this in a fun and loving way.
* A put-down is a low act; suggest to children that they become bigger with kindness.
* Teach solutions for common children's arguments or encourage 'special time' to recentre.
* Delay the use of screen technology, and be a good role-model in your own use of screens. Choose games and movies wisely for middle-years children. Limit screen time in balanced rhythms for a balanced life.
* Speak about the health implications of alcohol and smoking and similar topics in a natural way. Children are open to guidance after the 9-year crossing, laying a platform for teenage years.
* Inform children of stranger danger, but take care not to scare them unnecessarily.

CHAPTER ELEVEN
Let's Talk - Puberty

Many years ago, I was surprised when my 6 year old came home from school and commented, 'Hi Mum! We've been talking about virgins!'

I took a deep breath to compose myself. 'OK. What about virgins?'

His innocent reply: 'They don't have food on Virgin planes.'

Phew! My son was talking about planes!

Many parents feel anxiety when discussing puberty changes, menstruation and sex education, whatever their children's age and stage. I am often asked by parents when and how might they best introduce the topics of menstruation and sex. As I share ideas in parent workshops, you can hear a pin drop! There remains great uncertainty about these subjects.

Yet it is important that we are open to talking about puberty topics. If we wait until our children are teenagers we are often too late. And if parents don't speak up at the right developmental time, the internet and peers are very likely to take their place, with terrible results. We need to try to get past any awkwardness, embarrassment and uncertainty, take a deep breath, and view it as a wonderful opportunity to shed light on natural body processes and loving relationships. We cannot stay silent.

After an explanation of how to communicate to children at different developmental stages, this chapter will look at how we talk about puberty and bodily changes, especially periods. An understanding of periods is

Voice of a Menstrual Educator: Jane Bennett

During past generations, parents may have got away with staying silent about sex. Nowadays we cannot: with the internet it's like leaving them to the wolves.

helpful for both girls and boys, and most girls start having periods in the pre-teen years.

The second half of the chapter is about how and when we might talk about sex.

More than one conversation

It can be a relief to hear that there is no need for one intense talk in which you explain everything. At each stage of child development, seeds – pardon the pun – may be planted that make communication regarding menstruation and sex education almost effortless at the right time. This chapter explains what to say at each stage, and gives an overview of the 'unfolding' child, pre-teen and teen.

As parents are often lost for words, this chapter includes different parent and professional voices. It is my hope that, in reading the lines of others, parents will feel empowered to use their own voices.

While we need to be attentive to children's developmental stages, there is no exact 'right' timing nor is there one 'right' way to express things. Watch your own children and wait for signs.

Stages of child development

If sex education is important, does this mean we tell young children dry facts about sex? No. Ideally, we match words and conversations to children's stages of development.

Let's start at the beginning…

Early years

During children's first seven years of life, there are simple things parents can do to make later explanations of puberty and sex much easier. For example, having a relaxed and natural attitude to the human body. If parents feel comfortable with an open bathroom door, this means young children already know what is normal in an adult body.

In our family no one made a point of parading naked, but an undressed stroll to the bathroom and back was common, as was children popping in to chat while adults bathed. When my son was young he loved to bath with me, and it was in the bath together that we had our best chats about the amazing human body.

It is also helpful to call body parts by their real names right from when children are toddlers and these words are first needed. If we avoid words such as penis, vagina and breasts and replace them with child-like terms, such as 'doodle', then the real word and the body part may later seem rude, secretive, bad, shameful or a prompt for sniggering.

Young children can still be held in an innocent and imaginative world while giving body parts their appropriate labels and not being too worried about hiding them away.

Without overemphasising the point, we can say that the penis and vagina are special and sacred parts of the body. It is certainly much more helpful to see these body parts as blessed or special than to characterise them as rude or secretive. Sacredness can serve as an explanation for why we don't show these parts of our bodies in public.

When my children were around 7 or so, as an important step to protect them, I told them that it was fine to hold hands and have cuddles, but other people do not touch these body parts, as they are very special.

Describing periods in an imaginative and creative way can assist to normalise body processes and still hold younger children within their innocent stage of life. When my children were very young and asked what pads were for or saw menstrual blood, I treated periods as a normal part of life, not as taboo, and I believe this was helpful later on.

Young children are imaginative, so creative words are likely to be helpful for them. For children up to 9 years we can explain that period blood is different to the blood when someone hurts themselves, and that it isn't painful. My simple and imaginative explanation was that a period is 'the blanket from my womb coming out, as there is no baby inside'. I also nonchalantly mentioned from time to time that my daughter would experience her first period bleed when she was between 10 and 15 years old, and that we would celebrate this.

From natural observations and occasional chats, young children become accustomed to the notion of a boy having 'seeds' in his testes and a girl having an 'egg' with a 'blanket for a period' in her womb. These creative concepts may be brought to children in the middle years too if they haven't been introduced at a younger age.

There is no need to explain 'making a baby' until children enquire, and even then you can assess their stage of development and what they will readily understand. If children under 7 ask how a baby is made, it can be enough to say 'with love' and leave it there in a beautiful, wondrous space.

If the question is continuously asked after this age, the seed and the egg meet, and no more details are required. Interestingly, children who know that the seed and egg make a baby rarely ask how they get together. If they do keep asking, it is enough to say 'adult love joins the seed and the egg'. This response is still magical, dream-like and includes wonder, which is the right tone for a young age.

Voice of a Parent: Daniele

About a month ago my 5-year-old daughter asked me: 'Where do I come from?'

I took a deep breath and asked, 'What do you mean?', just to buy a bit of time to organise my thoughts.

She replied, 'What country am I from?'

I am thankful I asked, as she nearly got a very off-topic answer!

Middle years and teens

If children arrive at their middle years with a sense that bodies and their processes are normal, natural and not shameful, and with a sense that they have sacred body parts which they can clearly name, then they have a good platform for broader discussions. Between ages 7 and 12, children will still respond well to a sense of sacredness, to the idea that we can honour puberty changes, and to simple and imaginative insights.

Once children have grown into teenagers, then they are more capable of retaining dry scientific facts.

But we need to discuss puberty before the teen years, as most children in their middle years will go through puberty changes before then.

Puberty Changes and Periods

It is valuable for parents to be aware of natural body changes. Children are often blissfully unaware: the process of puberty may quietly unfold within them without anyone pointing out the changes or discussing them. It is best to let this happen and wait for children to enquire.

Puberty changes begin between the ages of 8 and 13 years. Transformations include an increase in body odour, breaking vocal cords for boys (girls' voices deepen too, but do not break), growth in body hair, enlargement of the penis and testicles in boys, and the development of breasts in girls.

I remember casually mentioning once when my children were young that I was unsure which hair grew first: pubic or armpit? I left it as a magical experience to wait and see.

Did you know that leg hair is the first to grow? It often thickens before pubic hair growth. If puberty changes are mentioned to children, such as pointing out their thicker leg hair growth, then they may become self-conscious and girls, for example, may ask to shave. It is best to leave children to discover changes for themselves.

They may ask questions about their body hair. Share interesting facts. Armpit hair, for example, naturally wicks the sweat from the skin for better ventilation. We have pubic hair to trap dirt and keep it away, just like eyelashes and nose hair.

Budding breasts may make nipples more sensitive, so some girls like to wear crop tops before they need a bra. Buying a first bra may be a good reason for a special day out.

Voice of a Parent: Lisa

My daughter asked to wear bras before it was necessary. I was wary of her growing up too soon. I suggested that she wear her dancing crop tops, and I reassured her that it would be worth the wait: once she did need a bra, we would go for a special girls' day out including lunch and bra shopping.

Voice of a Parent: Mel

We are generally a family with open doors when it comes to bodies. My eldest daughter was comfortable walking around the house naked well into her puberty changes, whereas my youngest daughter is the complete opposite. She has kept to herself, changing and showering behind closed doors from quite a young age. Both responses are completely fine and normal and we just respected each of them with their choices, but it's actually hard to believe that in this regard they are from the same family!

Starting periods

Preparations for periods and conversations about menstruation are necessary around age 10, turning 11. If a girl is developing early, then these ideas need to be introduced a little earlier.

Most girls start menstruation between 10 and 15 years of age. We need to be prepared for the girls who naturally start towards the younger end of that range, so that they do not feel isolated and alone.

It is common for girls of particular ethnic groups, for instance from Mediterranean and Afro-Caribbean origins, to start hair growth and menstruation at the earlier end of the range.

It might help to think of the age range for puberty changes as comparable to the age range for babies starting to walk in that some are early, some later, but it is not a competition and each age-start means nothing in the long term.

Voice of a Menstrual Educator: Jane Bennett

It is often stressful for the girl who is the first in her class to get her period, and similarly for the last boy in the class to begin puberty.

For girls in this situation, alongside giving ample emotional support, parents can let her know that she is the pioneer, and she will be able to help other girls when their time comes. Rather than feeling embarrassed and noticeably different, this can enable her to feel proud and empowered.

Voice of a Women's Health Practitioner: Melissa Gonella

We facilitate a privately run one-day programme for mothers and their daughters aged between 10 and 12 years of age. It's always best for the girls who attend to be 10 or turning 11. I've noticed that the girls turning 12 have often made a subtle shift in their awareness and tend to carry a more 'we know it all' kind of attitude. This can make them appear more resistant about discussions concerning the body, though they soften quickly and in the end they all have a positive day.

Stories of stressful menarche

Many women will recall personal stories of their shocked, difficult time at menarche (the onset of menstruation), having been given no previous information, awareness or knowledge from their mothers or other women.

Voice of a Parent: Veronica

My first period was a shock, as my parents had not informed me. I had to rely on my friends' bits of information, due to secrecy at home. I found the topic shameful and uncomfortable, to the point that I used toilet paper each month for the first year of menstruation, rather than telling my own mother. When I was around 14 or 15, she asked me, and I told her that I had my period. Finally I was able to wear period pads.

I was determined to be a more open parent. It has completely paid off: periods are viewed casually and supportively in our home, and by my son too.

Voice of a Parent: Kaz

I started my period when I was 13 and I had no idea what was happening to my body. I panicked and thought that I had somehow cut or hurt my vagina. When I asked my mum to help, she passed a little pamphlet into the toilet and that was all. I sat alone trying to make sense of what it said. I cried a lot.

My sister was two years older than me and I asked her why I had a period before her. She told me that she had had periods for two years now. I cried again, as I was so upset that this had been the first secret between us.

In the past (and still now to a certain extent), I believe some parents delayed educating daughters (and sons) about periods because they didn't separate talking about periods from talking about sex, and they wished to wait until children were older before they started discussing sex. I would strongly advise not confusing these two talks: girls need to hear loving and empowering voices on their own bodies and natural cycles of life before they enter into puberty. The discussions about sex usually come a few years later.

Voice of a Menstrual Educator: Jane Bennett

Given that we have three and a half to four decades of menstrual cycles, it is important to dignify the beginning of these years with positive information, emotional support and gentle celebration. Girls at this age are interested in their own bodies and those of other women, how they function and what they can do. Sex education has its own important place later on.

In sharing stories of difficult menarche, I aim to support and inspire parents to turn the tide and bring periods 'out of the back of a drawer', rather than shamefully hiding them away.

Girls are much better off if they are prepared beforehand, and they can be encouraged to support, accept, help and empower each other. This is a 'girl tribe'!

I recommend focussing on two areas when you are talking to daughters about menstruation before their first period:

1. The wonder of their bodies
2. How to be prepared

A feeling of wonder

I personally feel it is better for girls and boys to speak to real people rather than to be given or share a puberty book. If you feel you lack confidence or need more information, then do a little research beforehand and make notes to pass on as questions arise.

My feeling, and you can disagree with me, is that books may give too many facts, and include many areas at once, with information about sex and the reproduction system ahead of the time it is most needed. Seeing images of body parts may make children self-conscious about their body changes. Diagrams and explanations are hard to digest intellectually at this age. Cartoon pictures may devalue the body and appear comical, creating sniggers. All this can lead to a vague feeling of humour or confusion.

In contrast, parents themselves can explain key information with a sense of feeling, and leave pictures mostly to children's imagination.

Children like personal stories of when their mothers started their periods: they can genuinely relate to this whereas diagrammatic information in a book may seem distant and irrelevant to their lives.

Voice of a Menstrual Educator: Jane Bennett

Children of this age are highly unlikely to relate to or remember what they read or hear about periods if it is factual and descriptive, and there is no need for black-and-white sketches. Dry facts come later in the teen years and beyond. It is more important to instil a sense of wonder about how incredible the female body is. Avoid what I call 'the plumbing approach'. There are plenty of amazing facts about the menstrual cycle! And parents, please keep learning yourselves, for future questions and more 'Did you know...?' moments!

Did You Know...?

✳ Baby girls have all their eggs before they are even born: three to five million eggs to be precise! At birth, baby girls have one million eggs and by menarche (first period), they have between three hundred and three hundred and fifty thousand eggs in their bodies!

✳ An egg is the size of a full stop on a page or the little silver top of a pin.

✳ An egg is the only perfectly round cell in the human body.

Voice of a Women's Health Practitioner: Melissa Gonella

I use different-sized vegetables and nuts to show the size of the female reproduction organs. Did you know ovaries are the size of almonds and the uterus or womb is the size of a small pear? Amazing!

Children enjoy visual representation using real objects much more than looking at diagrams.

Voices of Jane Bennett and Melissa Gonella

The weeks of the menstrual cycle can be compared to a day–night cycle:

Week 1: We are naturally more tired and dreamy during the first 1–5 days of our period. (Day 1 is when bleeding begins.) This can be compared to night-time and sleeping. There is a natural need to rest and nurture ourselves, and if we don't get enough sleep then we are overly tired the next day.

Week 2: After the period has finished, we have an amazing capacity to multitask and get things done! We can compare this to the morning, when we are fresh as a daisy and can be very busy and focused on activity.

> Week 3: This is equivalent to the afternoon: it is a creative time for creative pursuits.
>
> Week 4: This is likened to evening energy and getting ready for bed. In week 4 of our cycle our bodies are getting ready for the next period. At this time we like order, routine, rhythm and good food. We may begin to feel tired.

The connection above between period weeks and times of day can also be linked to seasons of the year. Winter symbolises deep rest (like period days in Week 1); spring time is for new growth and a multitasking energy (Week 2); summer is a creative time (Week 3); autumn is an inward time and prepares for rest (Week 4 before the next period).

Women and girls who are aware of their menstrual cycle patterns often feel more connected to their own bodies. This means they may feel increased love and respect for their physical body. They may be less focused on their external looks as a source of their body's value.

Being prepared: practical information and pads

Listed below are common questions from children about periods and the answers suggest important points of information to cover.

What is a period?

A period has three stages: the first stage is that the womb creates a fresh layer of blood-rich membrane (the blanket), which is the body's way of preparing for the egg. Next, ovulation occurs where the egg (a full-stop-sized cell) is released from the ovaries (almond size) and travels down a thin fallopian tube to the womb (size of a small pear). The egg will break down with the unused blood-rich membrane: this is the period.

If a seed meets the egg, then a baby is created. It will grow in the womb for nine months. There are no periods during those nine months of pregnancy.

Why do we get periods?

The beginning of periods is about our bodies practising fertility – so that our bodies could have a baby once we're older. (Note that it can feel overwhelming if a 10 or 11 year old is told she has a 'woman's body' now. Consider instead using the phrase 'practising fertility'.)

How long is the time between periods?

A menstrual cycle can last for 24 to 35 days. All of this range is common and normal and the length of any girl's own cycle may fluctuate. For the first couple of years after menarche, periods are often more irregular, although some girls may immediately shift into a regular pattern.

How long will I bleed for?

Anywhere between three and seven days is normal. The first two days are usually the heaviest and then the blood flow is lighter. A first period may be as slight as a brown stain, with very little red blood, and any period can start with a slight brown stain before red blood.

How much blood is there?

Once periods are fully established, the total blood loss in one period is 35–50ml – about 2–3 tablespoons – not that much! (Note that girls often imagine there will be a lot more blood, so it can be comforting to explain this.)

How long do women keep having periods?

Until menopause, which occurs anywhere between the age of 45 and 55. At menopause, periods begin to be irregular – sometimes closer and sometimes further apart – and then stop altogether.

Do animals have periods?

Most mammals don't menstruate; however, many primates do, including lemurs, monkeys, apes and humans. A few bats and elephant shrews do too.

Voice of a Parent: Karen

When my 10-year-old daughter understood that the first period may be a small brown smudge mark in her underwear, she realised that her periods had already started. I enquired where the pants were, so I could wash them, and she said that the dog ate them!

Voice of a Menstrual Educator: Jane Bennett

Sometimes I meet girls who imagine that they will lose a litre of blood each period. It is good to paint a picture of how little blood there is.

There are some more questions from 10 and 11 year olds below. These come from a 'Celebration Day for Girls' – an event where children learn about puberty and menarche in a way that is fun and also respectful. The children at this Celebration Day could ask questions anonymously.

* *What do you say when you have your period?*
* *What if I get it at school?*
* *Do you always get your period at the same time of day?*
* *I have a book that says you get your period near your birthday.*
  Is that true?
* *Where were you when you got your first period and how old were you?*
* *Does every girl in the world have periods?*
* *Do animals go through puberty?*
* *Is it a good time to get a pet for yourself when you get your first period?*

(I smiled when I read this last question. I think this girl has been hanging out for an animal friend!)

School policy

Ask your child's class teacher and the school where girls can find menstrual supplies and what the policy is when girls need to go to the toilet during class if they are worried about their period coming. Is there a particular teacher they can talk to if they have concerns?

Most teachers and schools will recognise that children who are worried about their period coming, or about whether blood is leaking through their clothing, will be less able to concentrate on their learning. Schools are likely to have systems in place to support girls, or will set one up if contacted by a concerned parent. Girls need to be able to go to the toilet without having to ask and potentially be refused.

Voice of the Author: Lou

My daughter's class had a code word to use with the teacher when they needed to leave the room for a period-related reason. This idea came from the girls themselves, to make them feel comfortable having periods when at school. They spoke to their teacher, who was more than happy to play the game.

I advise parents to contact their girls' teachers to ask about a similar system of support.

Voice of a Parent: Kirrilee

After my initial conversations with my girl about menarche and puberty, I provided a simple writing book so she could share questions with me. It goes between our pillows. Sometimes it is easier to write a question than to speak.

Supplies of pads

It's great to prepare girls for their periods, and may have benefits beyond your own daughter if she can be helpful and supportive to her friends too. It can prevent girls feeling isolated, judged or different if they can talk about periods together among friends, carry supplies and develop a code word if one girl is in need.

Girls can choose or be given a little purse or bag for keeping a period pad or panty liner in their school bag, so they can feel prepared and won't be caught off-guard with their first period. It is a good idea while waiting for the start of menarche to provide panty liners, rather than proper menstrual pads, which may appear big and overwhelming, and are likely to be all that's needed until the period is established.

Perhaps buy a small calendar or diary so girls can note the start of each period, or find a code to use in their school planners. This will allow them to learn about their own rhythms as these unfold.

Girls like to choose their own purse, diary and panty liners, or a loving adult could gather these items as a gift before a more in-depth talk. You can include a special gift or note to remind the girl of her parents' love, always, amid the changes.

Voice of a Parent: Davini

I set up a special basket in the spare bathroom (which my children and their friends use) with a variety of pads and liners, so that all the girls had a supply and felt supported with their menarche and future periods while in my home.

Emotions

It is worth preparing girls for the mood changes that may occur before each period, and to watch for them yourself. Show compassion. Perhaps offer comfort at these times with warm wheat packs, foot spas, loving hair brushing and head massages. Give girls permission to feel emotions, and to find out what helps them alleviate distress. Perhaps they could try time alone quietly reading, journalling or doing something creative.

Voice of a Parent: Louise

The night before my daughter's first period she had an emotional rage and anger, and she didn't know why. It was surprising to the whole family. She even frightened her brother. We found her spaces to sit alone while she processed emotions – away from the family but still in our fold. The next day her first blood came.

Period pains

Some natural tips to help girls with period cramps:

* curl up with a heat pack or hot-water bottle,
* sip herbal tea (try peppermint or ask a practitioner about cramp bark herbs),
* ask a practitioner about supplementing the diet with fish oils and vitamin B1 or magnesium,
* massage the lower abdomen using massage oil with a couple of drops of lavender, clary sage or marjoram essential oil added to it.

Dads and brothers

Ideally, we need to create a home environment where dads and brothers feel comfortable when hearing conversations about periods, and when buying period pads as a normal part of shopping, so that there is a supportive and understanding environment around puberty across the gender divide. When dads disappear because it is 'Mum's territory', this sends a confusing message. Women need to help men and sons feel comfortable, for the sake of daughters and sisters.

Voice of a Menstrual Educator: Jane Bennett

Much has changed in this generation and girls are generally no longer 'left in the dark' before starting menarche. However, when we look closely, how included are dads? Is there still secrecy and an underlying shame around some areas of puberty, body changes, menarche and sex education? The last barrier is to make sure that the conversations include dads and brothers, at least some of the time. Do we unconsciously encourage girls to hide their pads or other evidence of periods from their father or brothers? If this is so, a girl will get the message that periods are shameful and they need to be secretive about them, even while we may be saying something else.

Voice of an 11 Year Old: Jo

If your parents are not together and you get your period at your dad's, how do you tell him?

Voice of a Teen: Mila

I teach my younger brother, who is 11, to look out for girls with their periods. If they have a blood mark on their skirt, he should offer his jumper to wrap around their waists.

A celebration

Girls may be offered a ceremony or a special meal out to celebrate their menarche (first period). This offer could be made while chatting to your daughter about future changes she will experience.

However, any social marking of menarche like this needs to be the girl's choice, and most often girls prefer a low-key family meal and not a ceremony. Make sure it is the girl's decision at the time rather than yours.

Do offer congratulations. (Dads can congratulate too.)

Mothers (or both parents) could, if this felt natural, write a letter at the time of menarche, to affirm that their love is unwavering throughout all the seasons and changes in life. The letter might include some wishes for their daughter's future.

In reality, times like menarche are hard to plan. Bring love and support and let the rest follow naturally.

Voice of a Parent: Tim

We talked about periods a lot with our daughter before hers started, and she saw period blood and pads openly. Her first period came while we were on holiday, and I was excited to take her out for a special meal. But she said, 'You two go, I'm in pain so I'll stay in bed!' I felt overjoyed that it was the beginning of her womanhood and bought her a special necklace.

Voice of a Menstrual Educator: Jane Bennett

Most girls experiencing their first period like to quietly adjust to the new experience, and it may be a bit much that there is a fuss on the day. However, a celebration can take place any time in the next few months when a girl may be more accustomed to her period. A special meal and warm congratulations is a wonderful message to give a girl.

In many cultures a ceremony to celebrate the start of menarche is the norm.

Voice of a Parent: Nira

In my culture (Hindu) we have a huge ceremony which friends, family and neighbours attend when a girl gets her first period. The girl is dressed in a beautiful new sari and sits cross-legged while women anoint her with sandalwood and turmeric paste on the sides of the cheeks and forehead, and also surround her with a smoking stick of frankincense. It is a blessing.

It reminds me of the three gifts at Jesus' birth: it is said that the 'gold' was the spice turmeric.

A new stage

Menarche can symbolise a new stage of life. This may be acknowledged with new freedoms and responsibilities. Some parents wait to offer ear piercing until menarche, as a symbol of a new stage.

Talking about boys' puberty

We have focussed on girls and menarche, as this is more likely to be a major issue in the middle years of childhood. But it is also valuable to acknowledge boys' transformation at puberty.

I feel it is important to bring boys' experiences to light, including so-called 'wet dreams', as some men report that they had no idea what was happening when these changes occurred in their bodies. We forget that boys, too, may be confused and left in the dark. A conversation in the middle years can be as simple as, 'In the future you may wake in the night with an erect penis and a new sensation. You will have practice experiences of your seeds. It may be a bit sticky, but it's natural and healthy, and we'll change the sheets.'

This creates a language around our sons' future journeys towards physical sexual maturity, and offers acceptance.

Let's Talk About Sex

A while after discussing periods and seeds with children, there is usually a sign. Children will indicate that they have questions or confusions about sex or reproduction. Or, you may hear children say words such as 'sex' and it is apparent there has been playground talk. Watch for the sign, wait for the opportunity, and be ready! It is often around the age of 11 or 12, and triggered by playground conversations. Parents will realise that a conversation about sex is required.

The first question to ask a child who is enquiring about sex or making babies is 'What do you think?'.

This question allows you to gauge where the child is within their own consciousness, and whether it is the right time to explain more about sex.

It is fine to say, 'What an amazing question!' and give yourself a few days to gather your thoughts, look up information and decide on how best to express ideas in a way which feels comfortable for you.

I offer here an example from my own experience of talking to my son, also to illustrate how the language I'd introduced when he was younger created a good basis for explaining sex when he was ready.

I was eagerly waiting for a sign. Rather than misinterpreted peer information, I was keen to include the sacred and love aspects to the topic of sex, not just the cold, dry facts of traditional sex education.

When my son asked me 'What does 'sex' mean, Mum?', I was ready. He had overheard a playground conversation when he was around 11 years old.

I responded, 'What do you think sex is?'

'When two people kiss and move their bodies around together,' was his innocent reply.

I knew it was time for a better explanation, as the playground talk would not diminish.

I questioned him on how he thought the seed and egg got together to create a baby.

His wonderful answer was that they met through the mouth when a boy and girl kissed.

'Not quite. Where are the seeds stored again?' I enquired lovingly. I could see him thinking it through. 'What is close to the store of seeds?'

His face was one of wonder, 'No way! They don't come out of the penis, no way!'

'And the egg, where is that near?'

He joined the dots to the physical act.

I believe it helped that I'd had a chance, before this topic became too embarrassing, to plant all the creative 'seeds' of information.

I painted the sacred into this new concept and aimed to teach about love and respect in sex. I explained that a baby was made not just by the egg and seed combining, but by love. I explained that when he was much older, to experience this level of physical closeness with someone is a real honour and great respect is required.

If we have powerful conversations in a positive and natural way, children tend to absorb the message, and then ask 'What's for tea?'.

Children usually assume at first that people only have sex to make babies. It's helpful if the first talk is simply the facts of life – how to make a baby – with respect and love as important ingredients at this time. Children of this age don't consider pleasure. You can discuss protection at a later stage of awareness and development.

Voice of a Parent: Lisa

When my 10-year-old daughter jumped on her 12-year-old brother in a playful sibling manner — a natural occurrence in our house — I was shocked by his new response: 'Stop sexing me!'

I waited a while to gather my thoughts. Then I talked to my son quietly, 'Today I heard you say, "Stop sexing me." What did you mean by that?' I asked without shame or negativity, just with curiosity. I wanted to know what he knew about this word.

My son explained that the boys at school had said to look the word 'sex' up in the dictionary and that it was between two people. He was 12 and I knew if I didn't speak and educate now, the playground conversations would continue.

I purchased a book about puberty and went through some of the themes from the book, and we had a chat.

His sister kept pestering to know too. In the end I gave up, as her curiosity persisted.

When I told her the same information about how the egg and seed met, she thought the physical process was gross and 'yucky'. In retrospect, she wasn't ready, and I needed to wait a while.

Voice of a Parent: Veronica

I have given my children snippets of age-appropriate information growing up, sensing when the time was right.

My friend was pregnant, and this became a natural catalyst for more conversations about conception and birth.

How to Talk About Pornography

Even though the topic of pornography may feel confronting to discuss in a book for parenting 7 to 12 year olds, we need to be on alert for the subject. It is best to be prepared. A Sydney study found 92 per cent of boys had been exposed to online pornography by the age of 16. The present generation of teenagers is the first to deal with the issue of pornography at this intensity and scale.

Why are so many teens (and even pre-teens) looking at pornography now? So many teenagers have screen technology that they use away from shared family spaces. If your teen does not have access to screens in their bedroom, they may still be exposed to images at a friend's house. Pornography on the internet is free and immediately accessible (this includes hardcore porn). Throughout the mainstream media more broadly, including movies and music, it is common for women and men to feature as sex objects and for the act itself to be shown as a performance. Pornography is becoming normalised.

Bestselling author Peggy Orenstein recently wrote an article for *The New York Times* titled, 'When Did Porn Become Sex Ed?' If sex education is not given in homes or schools in a natural, authentic and adequate way, tweens and teens may look to the internet to see what it is all about.

The media suggests that sometimes boys as young as 10 are encouraged to look at pornography by friends. It doesn't matter which school you attend or neighbourhood you live in, I would encourage all parents to be on the lookout for pornography, and be ready to have an empowering and loving conversation.

Again, I have an example from a parent to share. A boy aged around 14 years of age told his mother and father that people at school were watching porn.

This was his dad's concerned and caring response:

'I need to tell you that if you put pornographic images into your head, they are really strong and they will overstimulate you sexually. Those images will never leave your head. This is what could happen...

'You will be on the playing field at school and a girl's button will come undone and you will see the top of her bra. Because the images you've seen are overstimulating, you will get an erection.

'Also, you may start to see the girls you have known since primary school, who are your friends now, differently. With strong images in your head, it becomes easy to no longer see their personality, but just to see their boobs and legs.

'Most importantly, I really want you to experience a first relationship, a first kiss. If you put pornographic images into your head, you will not be with the real person during these experiences, you will be with the images instead. What I really need to say to you is this: the true enjoyment will come from *real* people, and not from images. So be very careful of these images or you may miss out on the *real* joy, the *real* passion, and the *real* love.'

(The boy's report back after this was that he warned his friend that if he kept watching pornography he might get an erection on the playing field and it would be embarrassing, and the friend stopped!)

I now share similar words during parenting talks and I know when I do that parents are sitting on the edge of their seats.

In the past, I worried about whether I should talk about pornography. Is it embarrassing for parents? But at the end of every talk parents thanked me. One dad, who was a police officer, told me that I needed to speak out. He explained that sexually related crime among teenagers and young adults had tripled in recent years in correlation with the increase in watching pornography. There is now a big drive to talk about the issue of consent. We need to speak to both genders. I do not wish to scare parents, but it is part of the world today and we need to be aware, to have the power and courage to change our teens' exposure, if need be.

I acknowledge that many parents find talking about sex (and particularly pornography) difficult and they don't know which words to use. We can't preach to teenagers, or condemn them: but we need to speak up. This is why I share heartfelt words. The underlying message is about developing love and respect. By having an open and sincere conversation at the right time with our teenagers, we may change perceptions of love, sex and relationships.

It is important not to shame teenagers' budding sexuality. Sexual curiosity and exploration is natural and normal. Rather than shaming anyone, my intention is to raise awareness of the effects of watching pornography and to encourage real, authentic and respectful relationships.

Voice of a Parent: Lisa

When my son was 13, we had the sex talk and I included the values of respect and setting boundaries. I felt it was important to do this, as I had heard that boys in his class were encouraging others to look up sexual words.

He had an awareness of different healthy and not-so-healthy foods, so I used this basis as an analogy towards sex too. I spoke about nourishing foods, which are so full of good stuff and really help people to have a healthy and happy body. I said that these foods can be compared to loving and respectful relationships and sex. I then described low nutritional or really unhealthy food, which is not good for the body at all and has disastrous effects if eaten long term. It doesn't nourish us to grow; in fact, it is not 'real'. I compared this to pornography and online images. He said he understood.

Voice of a Parent: Lulu

My son was 11 when he was told to type the word 'breast' into the family iPad, during playground talk. We found the word by looking at our recent search engine history. When asked, he said he didn't like what he saw and turned it off straight away.

Google has something called 'Family Link' which can be downloaded on all devices so that no adult content can be opened. Parents can access all online searches on any device linked to any family member, as well as the home computer or family iPad. It also shuts down the device after a designated period of internet use. It is a useful tool.

The benefits of talking openly

Talking with our children about their bodily changes, and later about loving sex, are rites of passage for parents. If we leave these topics to a book, teacher, sex education class or peers, the information is most often devoid of love and sacredness. There will be no ongoing natural conversation around these issues. When we do talk, we aim to bequeath to our children and teenagers a healthy relationship to their own bodies and to their natural processes. Being able to talk openly about these physical issues may indeed have far-reaching effects on our children's adult lives, including on future birth experiences. Research indicates that girls who are well supported during menarche go on to have a more positive body image, better self-esteem, healthier attachment to parents and peers, and easier birth experiences years later. (See S. Malony, 'How Menstrual Shame Affects Birth', *Women and Birth* (2010) 23, 153–159.)

Do you feel comfortable yourself with the topics of menarche, puberty, and later on sex and pornography? Please remember to take courage, and speak with your heart. Your children will feel more comfortable in conversations about these topics if you do. Take time to reflect on your own personal journey, and think through the issues that were difficult for you, so that you are ready to help them be more empowering for your children.

In Brief: Let's Talk - Puberty

Remember that bodies are natural. Use the correct names.

* An openness regarding periods is beneficial. Use imaginative verbal images rather than dry facts. 'It is the blanket from the womb, which comes out because there's no baby. It doesn't hurt.'
* Ask children 'What do you think?' when they ask you questions. Gauge their current awareness.
* Puberty is considered to be the physical stage between age 8 and age 18, before the fully fertile adult body is established.
* It is normal for a girl to have her first period anywhere between age 10 and age 15. The most common age is 12. The first

period may be very light and look simply like a brown stain. Periods can be irregular for the first three years.

* Create 'wonder' with amazing facts, as well as giving general information and practical advice. Be prepared with period pads.
* Prepare boys for 'seed' practice too.
* A talk about sex usually happens later than menarche and puberty changes. Wait for a 'sign' that children are ready and want to know more. Start by asking them questions. Intertwine love, sacredness and respect into descriptions of 'making babies'.
* Conversations with real people are often better than books as children will struggle to absorb dry facts and diagrams.
* Be ready to talk about the issues associated with pornography, if need be, and watch for signs. Try to address these in an empowering and loving way.
* Aim to provide a loving voice on the topics of menstruation, and later sex, to counteract the playground gossip. Take courage…

CONCLUSION
Looking Ahead...

CHAPTER TWELVE
The 12-Year Transformation and the Teen Years

This is a remarkable age: 12 signifies the end of middle childhood. During the five years before age 12, children transform on all levels:

* physical dexterity – consider their handstands and ball skills;
* intellectual development – at 12 they will have growing mastery over reading and writing;
* emotional awareness – the frontal cortex of the brain is developing;
* social and friendship connections will have become far more complex.

Then, at age 12, children embark on another amazing transition. The 12-year transformation involves body changes on a scale only seen before in the first three years of a child's life. It also signifies a further transformation of the child's 'I'. The 'I' is that part of our self that is our unique identity.

The transformation of our 'I' occurs in three stages:

1. as a toddler, children first believe 'I can'.
2. at around age 9, children feel 'I am alone'.
3. and now at 12, children realise 'I am an individual'.

The 12-year transformation signifies the beginning of a growing separation from parents, as children understand they are unique and different to other people – that they have their own 'I' – and as they strive to get to know their unique self.

While children go through this transformation, be prepared for the following three indications:

* a tendency to withdraw
* sudden criticism
* a striving for autonomy

It helps to understand these behaviours and tendencies in 12 year olds and during the teen years as part of the transformation in their individual 'I'. This chapter discusses each in turn, and offers suggestions for how we parents can respond.

A Tendency to Withdraw

After the 12-year transformation, children may begin to withdraw from close involvement in family life, and become more connected to their peers.

Moving away from parents towards peers is a natural progression. Your 12 year old may whisper in groups, and giggle with their friends behind closed doors. Whereas once you knew everything, now they will have secrets and plans you never hear about. Children are very influenced by friends in their push for independence.

Parents may be shocked and saddened when their child starts to withdraw and they lose physical closeness. The important message is that we don't need to feel alarmed or hurt. Time spent apart from parents is an important stage on the journey to adulthood. This is when teenagers work out who they are, as opposed to who their parents are, that they are truly unique from their parents.

I would encourage parents not to worry about an increase in time spent away from family life, behind a closed bedroom door. Teenagers need psychological space, and if we resist, they may need to push harder and move further away. Please try not to see withdrawal as personal; it's part of their stage of life.

Voice of a Parent: David

I have three teenage children and I had become so frustrated with all their closed doors, I was about to take the doors off at the hinges. But once Lou explained the stage of development, I understood.

Voice of a Parent: Martine

I am amazed how quickly my son went from being chatty to just grunting a greeting.

Voice of a 12 Year Old: Lucy

I'm not enjoying family bike rides so much any more. What's the point of starting at one spot and coming back to the same place? I'd rather just be at home now, unless it is a bigger adventure, to the city or something.

Staying connected

Don't be fooled by the invisible wall that may appear over time as children withdraw to their rooms, shudder at a parent's touch and ask not to be stared at if we even glance their way. Children after the 12-year transformation still require love. But not the same expression of love we give to younger children – this can feel stifling to a teenager.

So how do we display our love? The ideas below may help.

Sharing food

I recommend staying committed to the family dinner table. Teenagers will venture out of their rooms to eat! Make it a general rule that you sit and eat dinner together as a family, whenever that is possible. The evening meal is not to be taken to bedrooms. (This also means bedspreads won't be smeared with pasta sauce!) Eating together means there is a natural time of family connection built into the rhythm of every day. Even teenagers will find this reassuring! Cooking meals and laying the table signals the whole family's investment in this daily occasion.

Try to put all electronic devices away (including turning off phones and background TV) during the evening meal. Create an atmosphere of general chatting about each person's day. Perhaps lead the way by sharing your own day, rather than asking lots of questions. Older children will often join in if they're not repeatedly asked for information. (Questions can feel like an interrogation to some teenagers.)

At meal times, avoid the kinds of talk that teenagers might see as nagging, reprimanding or lecturing – create, as far as possible, a nag-free zone. Aim for low-key connecting.

In Chapter 4, 'Daily Connections', there are more tips for family meal times and a recommendation for the family dinner project, which has lists of conversation starter games to play with teenagers.

Create loving weekly and monthly rhythms

Children age 12 and beyond still enjoy family routines and rhythms, particularly those involving food! Perhaps commit to a meal out once a week or a pancake morning at home. My husband and our two teenagers share brunch together every Saturday in the same café. The waitress just says 'Usual?'. Consider a Friday pizza night, girls' movie night, once a month tenpin bowling… What will you all look forward to?

Touch

Some older children and teenagers love touch and offer up hugs every day. But most often, 12 year olds and teens subtly withdraw from touch.

Wait for occasions when teenagers agree to touch, perhaps when they have a headache, feel unusually tired or a little ill. When my daughter was a child, I stroked her head each night at bedtime. If she has a headache now, she will accept my offer of the same head rub. When her neck is tight from lots of homework or general stress, she likes a shoulder rub from her dad.

Little offerings

What is your 12 year old's favourite fruit? Leave it out from time to time for their arrival home from school. Or buy a little gift or trinket and leave it on their bed. Random acts of kindness express: 'I was thinking of you today' and 'You are important to me'.

Sharing interests

Join in with your 12 year old's interests: read your early teenagers' books, watch their movies, listen to their favourite music (let them choose the music for the car journey), and talk about it. I enjoyed reading the same teenage book series after my teenage daughter had finished it. We then chatted together about the plot.

Invest in activities where you and your teen share similar interests: going to concerts, outings, holidays and adventures, movies, food, and hobbies such as sport, cars, shopping and pampering sessions.

> ## Voice of a 12 Year Old: Zac
>
> I like to watch Friday night movies with Dad!

Expressing love

Even if the words aren't returned, I recommend still saying 'I love you' to older children and teens. Occasionally I say to my teenagers in a soft voice, 'Has anyone told you that they love you today?' This remark can be met with a grunt, a roll of the eyes, but at times with a loving 'I know you do' – and a smile. I also say, 'How is my favourite son/daughter today?' This is a family joke, as I only have one of each.

Be present when your older children moan about ailments or tiredness and maybe make a hot-water bottle. Assist them with homework when they are struggling or simply sit close by.

Try to start and end the day with kindness, with a feeling of warmth. Still whisper an 'I love you' or loving words before sleep (even though the time has come to knock on the door before going in to say goodnight.)

> ## Voice of the Author: Lou
>
> My daughter came with me on an overseas speaking tour. While we were away she received a text from her dad that read: 'I keep looking at the footpath to see if you're home yet. I must be missing you.' (My husband works from home and from his office desk he looks down the driveway to the footpath.)
>
> My daughter excitedly showed me the text, grinning from ear to ear. Seeing her face reminded me how important these 'random acts of kindness' are for our teenagers.

Connection from a distance

Recently I spoke with a friend who was upset because his daughter had chosen to live with her mother, so he was seeing her less frequently.

They had been very close during her childhood, so he was finding this distance very troubling.

I suggested he imagine his daughter each night, and join his heart to hers.

I know it can't take away the pain, but this exercise may transform the way we feel when we can't see our older children and teenagers, and change our outlook for the future.

Be there

The expression of love changes after the 12-year transformation and throughout the teenage years, but love can still be shown and grown. It's about timing and availability. Be present, so you can give support when asked. Give space, but keep a close and loving eye out.

I asked my husband for his main tip, and he simply replied, 'to be there'. I asked him to explain. 'To be around, to be present,' he replied.

We need to be there for our teenagers. Standing back, but observing. While teenagers seek more time alone as they are moving into adulthood, there is also the potential for depression and anxiety. Teenagers are often managing strong emotions, hormones, attitudes and peer group pressure. Parents need to distinguish between what is healthy and unhealthy isolation. If your teen's time alone appears to be unhealthy and you cannot bridge the gap, seek professional assistance.

Be careful of teenagers who are locked away with access to all media on their phones or gaming. If your teens use social media you will need to set boundaries on access, timing, contacts, hacking and bullying. I discuss this in more detail at the end of the chapter.

There may sometimes be a tendency for parents to let go as their children become teenagers, but this is very premature. Above all, our growing teenagers need to be loved and accepted, even though they are moving away from us and, at times, criticising us. The connection needs to remain strong. Never let go of the other end of the rope. They do not want us to let go, even when it appears so. Look at the suggestions above to form a strong foundation and bond to last throughout the teenage years. In their actions and manner, parents need to say, 'I am always there for you, but I give you space to grow'.

Sudden Criticism

After the 12-year transformation, children's capacity for judgements, discernments and critical thinking increases. They are trying to discover their own individuality and be true to their own uniqueness, so they look at their parents through critical eyes, and may be especially judgemental about our appearance and mannerisms. They are trying to work out who they are, as opposed to who we are.

It can be a real shock when children enquire, 'Are you really going to wear that outfit?' Or ask that you do not come to the school gate. You may wonder 'What has happened to make my children suddenly embarrassed about me?' Rest assured, it is normal. I recommend meeting this stage with humour and calmness.

> ### Voice of a 12 Year Old: Lucy
>
> My mum works at my school, but I do not see her or point her out to my friends.

Too far!

Try not to take critical comments from your growing children too seriously but if your teenager makes a personal critical comment that is actually hurtful and rude, it can be helpful for them and for you to show the reality of your feelings. 'I let many comments go, but that last remark actually hurt me.' Older children and teenagers are often quick to apologise and say they didn't really mean it.

Positive self-image

After the 12-year transformation, teenagers may turn their critical eyes on themselves too. They begin to compare themselves with others, or with an ideal image, and to judge their appearance.

It's important to give some thought to how we can encourage positive body image during this critical time.

With the growth spurt and bodily changes of puberty comes a deeper self-consciousness about the body, as well as a desire to play with different looks. Boys can become obsessed with hair gel and getting a new haircut, and girls often ask for earrings and nail polish.

It is normal for pre-teens and teens to become more focused on their looks as they start to express their individuality. Because they may be comparing themselves with media images that are often unrealistic, it is common for teens to be dissatisfied with aspects of their appearance. How do we encourage young people to make peace with their own unique and beautiful body type? Here are a few ideas.

Be a good role model

Try to be a good role model: avoid making negative comments about your body in front of children or teenagers. Consider the messages it may send if older children see a loved one fretting over their body, dieting or restricting food. Let's try to be loving to ourselves.

Display gratitude for all parts of the body. It is truly amazing!

Eat together

Sharing healthy meals together as a family means food is about enjoying company, as well as purely eating and good nutrition!

Enjoy exercise

As a family you can enjoy and encourage balanced exercise for how it feels, not to change how you look. 'I'm keeping my legs strong so they can carry me through life! Come join me!'

Criticise the media

Turn your young teen's critical eyes towards the media and its portrayal of bodies. Talk openly about the ridiculous notion of there being a 'perfect' body type, both for women and for men. Everyone's body fits them perfectly.

Point out when photos in magazines have been Photoshopped – most have!

Challenge the values surrounding young people, especially in the media: 'Imagine if everyone worried about shaping their hearts as much as their bodies: we would transform the world with kindness overnight!'

Set limits on clothing styles

While young people often enjoy expressing themselves and playing with their look, it's fine to set limits on sexualised clothing for pre-teens and teenagers. Skimpy or revealing clothing can make teenage girls overly conscious of particular body parts. No one is responsible for sexual harassment besides the harasser, but girls may not be ready for any inappropriate comments or looks sent their way.

Research Findings

A study conducted by Murdoch Children's Research Institute and the University of Melbourne involving 1,100 girls and boys aged 8 and 9 found one third were unhappy with their bodies.

This is concerning – age 8 and 9 is very young to be expressing this dissatisfaction. We need to be realistic about the nature of bodies and to talk about all body types in a positive manner with children of every age.

Being seen

Although there is a tendency to self-criticism, 12-year-old children also want to be seen, and to be recognised in a new light. In many Steiner-Waldorf schools, children at this 12-year transformation time are 'the leaders of the light' during the Winter Festival, and walk on stilts for a circus performance. The rest of the school literally looks up to them!

Criticising our views and opinions

With a new capacity for judgement and comparison, children during the teenage years may roll their eyes at parents' opinions as well as at their appearance.

Older teenagers may build strong opinions and adamantly contradict their parents' lifestyles and beliefs. Teenagers have to deconstruct before they construct and centre their own views. This is an important stage in the development of critical thinking. If young people are unable to explore this critical process, there is a risk they may 'fail to launch' into adulthood, resulting in long-term dependence on their parents. They may not develop confidence in their own independent decision-making or fully take on their own individual responsibilities. Criticising our opinions occasionally is about our children gaining the ability to think for themselves.

What can we do to help with this stage?

* Listen more. If a teenager feels unheard or undervalued, they argue back or withdraw.
* Ask teenagers' opinions and ideas, so they feel valued and counted.
* Ask teenagers about what they are interested in. 'What is your favourite song, colour, food?' is a good conversation game for car journeys.
* When your own opinions don't align with your teenager's, don't take it personally.
* Don't expect consistency: teenagers may try on views like outfits, to see which ones fit.
* Challenge teenagers to use critical thinking to work through their ideas.
* Without asserting they change their mind, point out gaps between the views they are expressing and the family values they live inside at home.
* Listen to their view and then quietly state your own: 'This is my take on it … '.

Parenting beyond the 12-year transformation and through the teenage years requires the best of who we are as adults. We will be challenged at every level and our integrity will be questioned. We are forced to be conscious, compassionate, and honest with ourselves too.

Celebrate differences

Each family member's temperament is unique. During my workshops, I jokingly ask parents to raise their hands if they received the child they expected. There is usually a ripple of laughter and no hands go up. A parent can be extroverted and their teenager introverted, or vice versa. A parent may love sport and their teenager may be happiest sitting still and reading.

If we constantly try to mould teenagers into who we expect them to be, they may struggle to accept themselves later in life and therefore to experience self-love. Let your teenager's temperament unfold. They are sure to be different to you.

A critical eye on the world

After the 12-year transformation, older children and teens turn their critical eyes out towards the world. They show concern and shock at the unjust systems they see, and the unfairness of racism, sexism, poverty and the hardship of others. They are concerned with animal abuse and unsustainable living practices. Teenagers are rightly critical of all that could be changed for the better. They are the pioneers for social and environmental change in the future.

Voice of a Teen: Mimi

One of the things that I would change is all the disrespect and hatred in the world today. Treat people the same, no matter what they look like. Kindness is one of the most important qualities to have. If everyone showed kindness, I believe our world would be a much happier place.

Striving for Autonomy

With the development of their individual self, there is a natural drive in teenagers for greater individual autonomy. After the 12-year transformation, teenagers ask for wider physical boundaries and greater independence from parents.

Voice of a 12 Year Old: Zac

I'm allowed to ride my bike on the footpath around our local park from our house. Soon I hope I can ride all the way to the library with friends.

Voice of a 12 Year Old: Lucy

If my mum pops to the shops for five minutes, I always have to go with her. She won't leave me at home. I hope I can stay at home alone for short periods soon: I know I can be trusted.

Inner autonomy

It is not only the physical boundaries that are being stretched; after the 12-year transformation, young people have a deep unconscious desire to find inner autonomy from parents — which in simple terms means that they find it hard to be told what to do! Their growing intellect combined with a new sense of autonomy means teenagers argue their point.

Teenagers may have an inner drive to do the exact opposite of what parents say, so that they can feel they are thinking for themselves. If a parent wakes up on a cold morning and says to a teenager 'put your coat on', the teenager is likely to feel an immediate inner barrier to following the instruction because staying warm wasn't something that arose as their own independent thought. So with growing autonomy may come growing rebellion. It is handy to know this!

New creative discipline techniques

How can parents negotiate with their teenagers given their inner resistance?

Our creative discipline techniques require change after the 12-year transformation. Here are some suggestions to reduce conflict with your teen:

* Check in. If there is enough trust with your teenager, change your phrasing so you are checking in rather than instructing. For example, ask 'Got a grip on the weather?' rather than saying 'Put your coat on.' A question may be more productive than a direct command.
* Communicate during non-confrontational times. Talk calmly, away from the heat of the moment.
* Go for win–win. Find a compromise together.
* Use humour.
* Let them negotiate. Teenagers will usually respond, 'OK, I'll do what you ask, after I've done...' This is fine, but let them know that their actions need to match their words in order to maintain their integrity and your trust.
* Use 'I' statements rather than 'you' statements. For example, 'I'm worried that you won't get your homework in on time, and it will cause added stress' rather than 'You are not studying, when are you going to do your school work!'
* Use minimal words. I learnt the hard way that NAG stands for Not A Good idea. Once you have made a reasonable request, if your teenager ignores it, repeat the request in a single word. For example, just say 'Clothes', if you've already asked them to tidy their room. Teenagers love to argue, so minimise words.
* We know what happens when a bull in a china shop meets another bull in a china shop... Stay calm, and a teenager's mood may dissipate.

Healthy boundaries and teenagers

Teenagers still need limits, even though they are pushing the boundaries and asking for increased autonomy. New challenges arise during the teenage years, which require thoughtful actions, guidelines and new limits.

Boundaries are not about control for the sake of it. Teenagers need to feel the love and care behind limits, and that ultimately you are looking out for their best interests. The benefits of boundaries include:

* allowing teenagers to grow at a slower pace.
* minimising the consequences of teen recklessness.
* teaching teenagers to consider life from different perspectives.
* helping teenagers learn negotiation skills.
* letting teenagers know that they are loved.

Here are some examples of the kinds of boundaries it is worth instilling with teenagers:

* **Regular sleep patterns.** Teens may need prompts to go to bed, and I also make casual remarks about the issues caused by lack of sleep. These difficulties include that the immune system is weakened, and concentration is impaired, not to forget the occasional mood swing!
* **Limiting exposure to social media.**
* **Following the guidance of movie ratings.** Wait for the appropriate age before viewing scenes of violence or sex, which can never be removed once seen.
* **Healthy food choices.** Excess sugar can lead to headaches and a rollercoaster of emotional lows and highs.
* **Safety and accountability** – especially ensuring that parents always know where teenagers are.
* **Monitoring exposure to alcohol and drugs.** Ask questions about teenage parties, and insist on being able to drop them off and pick them up. Have natural family discussions about the effects of binge drinking and drug taking.
* **Avoid immediate material gratification.** If teens want a large material item, suggest that they wait for a special occasion or that they work to pay for it themselves.
* **Family values.** While it's fine to express emotion, including negative emotion, put-downs or words that upset others require limits. There needs to be an expectation that as a family we look after each other, even though disagreements arise from time to time.

✳ **Contributions to household life.** Teenagers are part of the family team, and are expected to be responsible for some chores.

Parents can't simply declare boundaries for teens. We need to invest time and energy explaining the value of each limit and discussing its purpose. With teens, it will be easier if we talk, share and listen rather than lecture. This lets them get a feel for the limit, and then later self-regulate their own behaviour once they learn the value of the boundary.

I once read that when we set limits for teenagers, our effectiveness depends only 25 per cent on what we say but 75 per cent on how we say it. See and hear their side of the issue. Ask questions, and really listen to their communication.

Boundaries ideally need to be set in a loving and relaxing – sometimes even light-hearted – environment. I know this is not always possible! For my family this is usually around the dinner table. I don't think I have ever used the word 'boundary' with my children; we just discuss how to be safe, healthy and part of our family team. Setting limits can be enjoyable at times, as it allows for a greater connection. Negotiation of these issues begins the journey of your chidren's transition into adulthood.

Limits need to be revised and extended as teenagers mature.

Of course our teenagers are likely to push boundaries, and may occasionally sulk and say that their friend's life is easier or is subject to fewer limits. There may be misunderstandings, and also mistakes on both sides. Setting boundaries is not always easy or simple, but loving boundaries say: 'I am interested in you; I care for you.' Teenagers need to sense that boundaries are fair, and that they arise from love.

I asked my daughter how she felt about the above boundaries, and her response was 'Ask me when I'm 20, no teenager is ever going to say give me more boundaries!'

Teenagers naturally grow in autonomy, but that doesn't mean that parents are helpless bystanders; it's an invitation to reinvent your relationship together.

Throughout all the changing dynamics, what teenagers need to hear from a parent is: 'I am on your side, now, always and forever.'

Phones and social media

After age 12, children may be travelling on public transport alone, or walking to or from school, and parents may decide now is a good time for their first phone. Consider buying a basic phone: there are still handsets without cameras, internet access, games, and so forth. These offer connection to you and to friends without the difficulties of social media or constant internet access.

Providing a phone or any device with access to the internet and social media has its risks unless parents set certain boundaries together first.

At some point, older teens often want to join different kinds of social media. This is an extension of their strong sense of connection to their peer group. Social media has benefits: it can lead to a sense of belonging with peers, family and community, and a sense of immediate connection with loved ones. It can bring extended family closer together, such as cousins and grandparents.

However, there are dangers, so parents need to have family conversations. The risks include seeing upsetting or disturbing content, witnessing online bullying, or being contacted by strangers. Come up with guidelines and agree on specific rules. Say that you trust them, but all people, adults included, need to be wise and savvy when online. Here are some key topics to open up discussions with your teenagers about keeping safe online, and establishing clear boundaries.

* Advise them to take a screen shot and show you if anything they see online is disturbing.
* Explain why they mustn't take or send photos of other people without permission, or share photos of themselves that they wouldn't be comfortable showing to you. They need to understand how to manage their digital footprint with integrity.
* Discuss online bullying, and how much easier it is to text something nasty than to say the same words to someone's face. Say you know they are not likely to do this, but that no negative talk will be tolerated, as this is cyberbullying.
* Discuss stranger danger online, and the importance of not speaking to anyone they don't know. Discuss what your teenager should do if they are contacted by someone unknown, and advise them to show you immediately.

* Tell them not to click on any buttons or links or advertisements that pop up while they're online.
* Explain that while your teenagers are learning to use their phones or family iPads responsibly, you will check their devices from time to time.
* Ensure your security settings avoid adult content.
* Parents can join social media platforms too, and this is a good idea in the teenage years.
* Set limits on where devices can be used (in the family area at first), and when. Consider having a maximum length of time for looking at a screen. To reduce the impact on young people's sleep it helps to leave phones outside the bedroom at night, and to have a wind-down screen-free period before bedtime.

Note that the World Health Organisation now lists internet gaming disorder as a mental health condition.

Families can agree together on the limits and write up a contract before phone or social media access is given. Make it official. The boundaries can be loosened in later years if teenagers prove responsible.

Ideally, hold off as long as you can. However, in my opinion, it is better in the long run to educate teenagers about technology and social media once parents feel their teenagers are responsible enough to adhere to the limits and understand the risks, rather than to ban access to devices completely. Regulating with firm controls rather than prohibiting creates trust. Otherwise, older teenagers often find a way to accces screen media anyway, and parents have then lost the power to educate and to reinforce values of safety, health and respect.

Voice of a Parent: Lisa

I thought I was doing the right thing by saying no phones after 7 pm in time for bed, but I was shocked to read that it takes two hours after blue-light exposure from a screen to re-regulate the production of melatonin (the sleep hormone).

A New Stage for Parents and Teenagers

As our children go through the 12-year transformation, we as parents are likely to also be entering into a new stage of our lives as our parenting role shifts. It is a time to rediscover ourselves. Remember your own youth – your teen years and beyond. Show your young people photos of your adventures. It's good to share your past passions and life in your teenage years and twenties: it helps them to see you as a person, before becoming a parent. For a second or two, they may feel that you are cool too. Or that you were once!

Voice of a Family Facilitator: Kurt Shean

Around the 12-year transformation, or during the early teenage years, I encourage parents to share personal stories with their young teens. We ask:

* What is the most amazing sight you have ever seen and what made it so special?
* Who are the man and the woman you most admire and why?
* What's a big challenge you've overcome in life and how did you do it?

It is wonderful to witness the strengthening of family bonds through positive stories.

It can be difficult for parents to adjust to their children's changing lives. For some, the sense of not being needed so much, or not in the same way, can bring sadness. For others, there may be an increase in career pressures. Parents may have more time than they did five years before, which means there is space for finding passions and purpose, for redefining ourselves. We are growing in self-development too, alongside our children.

Be kind to yourself as a parent; judge yourself less. Being less self-critical may mean you will also be less critical and more accepting of your changing teen.

I often ask my husband how he feels our teenagers are going. He always replies, 'Ask me when they're 22.' Once they are in their 20s, our children will return to us in a new way. At that stage, you will see less of the three indicators of teenagehood I have discussed in this chapter (a tendency to withdraw, criticism of you, a need for autonomy). They will start to see us as human beings, as well as parents.

Rudolf Steiner emphasised:

> It is of great importance to know what happens at certain points
> of a child's life and how you should act with regards to it, so
> that through your actions you may radiate light onto the child's
> whole life.

At 12, our children are still children, yet an inner change is required of them. They are transitioning to the teenage years. This is a daunting, challenging and exciting time, for both parents and children. My son once asked me, 'Why do people say the word "teenager" with a negative tone?'. It stopped me in my tracks. I had to agree with the question: why do they? Teenagers are passionate, loyal, dynamic, creative and humourous, among many other positive traits. I enjoy being around them. We need to understand their world and their inner changes to strengthen our connections. It is my sincere aim that we all look forward to our children's teenage years with growing awareness and confidence.

This is the end of this book, as we have travelled together through parenting children from 7 to 12 years. I hope you have gained new insights, and many practical ideas to enhance family life during middle childhood.

In Brief: The 12-Year Transformation and the Teen Years

* After the 12-year transformation, children tend to withdraw more to find themselves.
* Stay connected at the dinner table, with joint activities, and with random acts of kindness.
* Critical thinking develops, and this may be aimed at parents' dress sense!
* Celebrate different temperaments in the family.

* It is normal for teenagers to feel a growing autonomy: they not only push against physical boundaries, they will push against parents' instructions too.
* Guide rather than tell. Negotiate and communicate.
* Boundaries are required for sleep, health, chores, media and more…
* Teenagers need to feel that you are always committed to them, that you are saying: 'I am on your side.' 'I love you always, through all the changes in life.'
* Reinvent your relationship with your teenagers, it will be worth it! They are amazing!

Meet the Author

Lou Harvey-Zahra is an experienced parenting coach and respected author of many holistic parenting books. She grew up and did her teacher training in England before moving to Australia where she has taught in numerous kindergarten, primary, special needs and Steiner-Waldorf school settings for over 25 years, including training teachers.

Lou runs conscious parenting workshops, online parenting courses, and presents to parents and teachers across the globe. She is a mother to two grown-up children and currently lives in Melbourne, Australia.

Visit Lou's website happychildhappyhome.com and follow her on Instagram (@HappyChildHappyHome), Facebook and YouTube (Happy Child, Happy Home).

Also by Lou Harvey-Zahra:

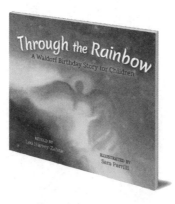

The birthday story has been told for generations and holds a unique place in the hearts and memories of thousands of families. *Through the Rainbow* is a faithful and inspiring retelling of the most well-known version of the story by Lou Harvey-Zahra, and is accompanied by soft, ethereal illustrations by Waldorf artist and teacher Sara Parrilli.

Discover more inspiring parenting books:

Learn how to make ordinary family moments extraordinary, understand important stages of childhood, positively transform everyday behaviours and maintain happy relationships in these practical, accessible books.

Happy Child, Happy Home introduces the concept of 'conscious parenting' as a way of helping any family home become more fun, connected and harmonious. Chapters include positive ideas for play, rhythms and routines, storytelling, craft, exploring the twelve senses and more.

Creative Discipline, Connected Family includes ten practical tools to help parents solve everyday issues such as fussy eating, bedtime struggles, sibling sharing, tantrums and anger, while fostering positive, lifelong family connections.

 Also available as eBooks

florisbooks.co.uk

Practical advice and activities for family rhythm:

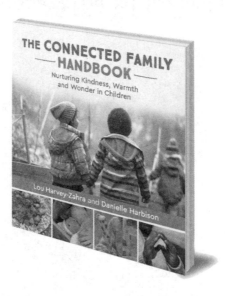

In this unique and inspiring book, parenting coach Lou Harvey-Zahra and parenting blogger Danielle Harbison offer empowering advice and practical activities for carers of toddlers to ten-year-olds.

Lou and Danielle explore ten important themes for families: Kindness, Home, Mealtimes, Movement, Warmth, Teamwork, Adventure, Nature, Wonder and Celebration. They suggest ways to weave each theme into family life through easy crafts, fun recipes and engaging stories and verses. They also share tips on creative discipline, positive play and establishing enjoyable family rhythms and routines.